DEFYING DESPAIR

Feed the Mind
Train the Body
Nourish the Soul

Anthony Scelta Jr.

MYSON PUBLISHING
FLORIDA

MYSON PUBLISHING
POMPANO BEACH, FLORIDA

Designed by Irene Archer,
www.book-cover-design.com

Printed in the United States of America
ISBN 0 - 9745874 - 0 - 0

CONTENTS

Part III: *The Physical Challenge*

FOREWORD

There has been an explosion of books on Parkinson Disease, including two of my own: *Shaking Up Parkinson Disease and 100 Questions and Answers about Parkinson Disease.* About half of the books are by doctors giving patients and care-givers information on treating Parkinson Disease, and about half of the books are by patients giving information on coping with Parkinson Disease. Why is this book different? It's different because Anthony Scelta was diagnosed with Parkinson Disease before he was 25 years old! He has lived a life, for all intents and purposes, knowing only Parkinson Disease, with a brief memory of what it was like to live without this malady. Most people in his shoes would have drowned in despair. Anthony has not! Somehow through will, through physical conditioning, through sheer "guts" he gives all of us a message of hope in adversity. This is definitely a book worth reading!

Abraham Lieberman, MD
Internationally recognized expert on Parkinson Disease, author of five books on the topic, and National Medical Director of the National Parkinson Foundation.

INTRODUCTION

Out of the one and a half million Parkinson's sufferers in this country, I am one of the few to have developed the disease by the age of twenty-five. Before I reached thirty years of age, I displayed most of Parkinson's worst symptoms, including debilitating fatigue, extreme rigidity with muscle spasms, slowness of movement, tremor, and insomnia. While dealing with the emotional issues of having a failing body, I needed to handle the practical problems of being the single dad of a newborn. Adding insult to injury, my disability prevented me from continuing my livelihood as a personal trainer. Flat broke, overwhelmed, and despondent, I sank into the abyss. This invisible foe called Parkinson's Disease had dismantled my life. At my darkest moment, I knew I had to make a decision: Give up on living altogether and waste away, or fight to get my life back.

I chose the latter. But who was I fighting? How does one fight an insidious and intangible adversary like Parkinson's Disease? I didn't know exactly how, at first, but I was determined to prevail. No matter what, I would not let it beat me. Instead, I would defy it!

Earlier in my life, the solution to most of my problems was somehow always related to fitness—my whole world revolved around it. Fitness, in one form or another, was my livelihood, my source of self-esteem, and my passion. If I was going to defy despair, exercise needed to play a big role. However, in the poor physical condition that I was in, it was hard to fathom ever being fit or even simply feeling good again. I realized that training my mind, as well as my body, was the only way I would truly feel whole again. That is when my spiritual journey began.

After much exploration, study, and reflection, I realized that three essential ingredients in facing monumental challenges are Faith, Inspiration, and Tenacity. With the insights that I gained, I built a foundation of inner-strength to face what was before me. Suddenly, my obstacles were no longer barriers, they were challenges. As my mind was getting stronger, my body was following suit. The mind-body connection was more profound than I had anticipated. The realizations that I made through study and introspection were helping me emotionally. Additionally, my new outlook allowed me to fight past my physical limitations in order to strengthen my body. Becoming fit, in turn, further fortified my emotional and mental state. It was a powerful cycle that gave me my life back.

Now it's time to create your own success story. Defying Despair can help those who want to:

1. Find meaning in their lives, particularly in their suffering.

2. Overcome any adversity while reveling in the good things that life has to offer.

3. Strengthen their mind, body, and spirit.

4. Feel healthier and fitter than ever before.

Part I of the book contains a light-hearted account of my struggles with Parkinson's, and the events leading up to my metamorphosis. From denial to depression, this section describes my experiences with the same issues that plague all of us during times of crisis.

Part II sets forth the cerebral portion of my mind-body strategy for defying despair. In it, you will learn to be F.I.T., by building a foundation of Faith, Inspiration, and Tenacity. Whatever the source of your despair—divorce, illness, loss of a loved one —you will discover that all of us have the same battle to fight. Despair is our common enemy, and the F.I.T. strategy is the common battle plan.

Part III describes the role physical fitness plays in preventing and managing illness. The emphasis of this part is on the benefits of exercise, and how it can strengthen the mind as well as the body.

Part I:

The Harbinger Of Despair

Chapter One
The Bomb Drops

Plan To Be Surprised

"When we make plans, God laughs." I heard this Jamaican proverb many years ago, but at the time, I paid it no mind. You see, in my early twenties, I had it all planned out. As far as I knew, nothing could stop me from personal training clients, having fun, and basically flying by the seat of my pants. Vibrant, and in peak physical condition, I wanted to enjoy life to its fullest. I was young, brash and seemingly invincible—I didn't think there was anything beyond my reach. That's when God let out a guffaw that sent a shockwave through my life. My life's vision had been snuffed out, and replaced with a nightmare that was unimaginable. Despite all my planning, developing Parkinson's Disease at the age of twenty-five was definitely not something I had anticipated.

My first symptom was tightness in my left shoulder and arm. I was even having difficulty putting on a jacket because of it. At the time, I figured it was nothing more than a minor, sports-related, shoulder injury. Shortly after I experienced my first symptom, something happened at the gym. In between sets of a shoulder exercise, my whole body started to tremble. My legs were so wobbly that I could hardly drive home. I figured I must have been glycogen depleted—when the body is deprived of sugar—due to overexertion. Within days of that incident, my left hand started to tremble quite visibly, for no apparent reason. I didn't know what the heck was going on. All I could think of was that I had developed some sort of sensitivity to caffeine. So I eliminated it from my diet. Finally, on one occasion, during a heated repartee between me and a crooked car salesman, my left arm shook very violently and uncontrollably. It was then that I decided to see a doctor.

The first doctor I saw dismissed my symptoms as "probably stress related," but tested for a possible thyroid condition just in case. When hyperthyroidism was ruled out, and my tremor persisted, I was referred to a neurologist. Like a Ping-Pong ball, I was bounced from one specialist to the next. Comments like, "You're okay, you're probably just depressed," coupled with questions such as, "Are you gay?" made the process terribly frustrating. What on God's green earth did my sexual orientation have to do with anything?

Then came the real fun and games—the testing. First, I went for an MRI, then for a CAT scan, and then for another MRI. These exams were my own little tubular tunnels of torture: Forty-five glorious minutes of being entombed in a temporary casket, with loud thumping noises walloping my eardrums. If I would've known then that the torture tunnels would be the most pleasant of all my tests, I might have tried to enjoy them more.

A nerve conduction test, called an EMG, was by far the most harrowing of the lot. Before the test even started, I knew I was in trouble. You know how it works. When the doctor tells you, "This won't hurt a bit," you know it's going to hurt. If he says, "This may hurt a little," it's going to hurt a lot. Well, the doctor performing the EMG said to me, "This is going to hurt quite a bit." So you do the math.

During this procedure, I was given the opportunity to do my best impression of a voodoo doll. First, the doctor would stick a large needle into a particular muscle in my arm—the muscle between the index finger and the thumb, for example. Then I had to tense up that muscle, and hold it for about thirty to sixty seconds. So, while the needle was jabbed between my index finger and my thumb, I was told to make a fist. The pain was excruciating. After being probed approximately thirty more times, in various parts of my arm, it was almost over.

By then I was exhausted, and severely nauseated. But the fun continued for another half hour, with unbearable electric impulses being applied to the same traumatized parts of my arm. At least if I ever get electrocuted, I'll be prepared. When I was done being tortured, I was hoping they could at least tell me something; anything. But they couldn't.

A year of more probing and testing finally led to the initial diagnosis. Frankly, I thought the doctor was nuts. Besides, he didn't even sound convinced of the diagnosis himself. Believing that the diagnosis had to be wrong, I got three more opinions, the last of which was given by a renowned doctor at the National Parkinson's Foundation in Miami. At that point, I finally believed it.

The unequivocal words, "You have Parkinson's Disease," left me numb. As I left the office, I replayed the doctor's description of the illness in my mind. "It is a progressive, neurodegenerative disorder that eventually leaves the patient debilitated. And there is no cure." In essence, part of my brain was dying, and there was nothing they could do to stop it. It was just too surreal to process. I wasn't scared, sad, or angry; just totally stupefied.

Breaking the News

That night, when the time came to tell my girlfriend of the official diagnosis, the stark reality of the situation hit me like a ton of bricks. I had heard the doctor utter those two dirty words that afternoon, but somehow, when "I have Parkinson's Disease" came out of my own mouth, the realization set in. I had never uttered those words before. There was always that suspicion, or hope to be precise, that the first three doctors were wrong. But I had finally run out of wiggle room. There were no more "maybes." I had Parkinson's Disease....period. That night, my girlfriend and I, both cried ourselves to sleep.

Mustering up the courage to tell my older brother and my mother didn't come until a week later. My mother made an effort to be strong, and offered many supportive words. My older brother, however, went into immediate denial, despite the second, third, and fourth opinions. It was his only way to cope with the pain. I actually waited an entire year to tell my father, fearing he wouldn't be able to handle the situation. Despite the immense pain he must have felt upon hearing the news, he hid it fairly well. For him though, my particular condition was especially hard to accept. All my life, my body and athleticism had been a source of great pride for him. It was a rare occasion for him not to "feel my muscles" during one of our visits. So he had to get used to the fact that his son was no longer that guy with the muscles. For me, the pain my illness was causing my loved ones was much harder to bear than the disease itself. Outside of my family, I only told my closest friends.

It was very strange, but every time I broke the news to someone, I felt as if I was letting them down. It felt like I was telling them that I just paid off a gambling debt with the deed to their house. I think it's common for people who become ill to feel guilty in some way. Whether my feelings came from the guilt of not being able to fulfill certain expectations, or from the guilt of causing other people pain, or something else entirely, I do not know. It was probably all of the above. This guilt, however, was only a harbinger of the many extra burdens to come.

Assimilating the Unimaginable

The future was suddenly uncertain and ominous. I could no longer entertain pie-in-the-sky fantasies of all the great conquests that were in store for me. Instead, they would be supplanted by the realities of surviving day-by-day. I handled the next few weeks relatively well, considering the doctor's diagnosis occupied my every waking and sleeping thought. It was literally overloading my brain.

But, I am invincible

Then, suddenly, after a few weeks, I became totally at ease. I barely gave my condition a second thought. I guess my mind just shut down, in a sense. With this, came a new attitude. For some reason, I could not fathom being affected by this disease—or anything else for that matter. Not only was I physically fit, but my symptoms were minor. And after I was prescribed my first medication, I felt even better. To my delight, the tremor and stiffness had been minimized. In my mind, no obvious symptoms meant no disease.

I guess my attitude was to be expected. After all, I spent twenty-five years thinking I was invincible. Why should that change in just a few weeks? My past was replete with stupid stunts, all of which left me unscathed. So who could blame me for thinking my good luck would continue?

When I was a teen-ager, a friend and I used to get drunk, and speed through New York City's Central Park in the middle of the night. Most of the time, one of us would be hanging half-way out of the sun roof. How we didn't fly out of the car taking sharp turns at 70 mph is a mystery to me. Years later, when I was in Costa Rica, I also exhibited poor judgment that put my life in danger. Very late one night, I was roaming the streets in search of a particular discotheque that was located in an extremely dangerous area, especially for tourists. It was so bad that even the cab drivers wouldn't stop in that neighborhood. So being as prudent as I was, I attempted to find the club--on foot. I never found it, which meant my stay in the bad part of town was brief. Luckily, my arrogance didn't get me killed that night.

These examples provide only a glimpse into the moronic adventures of "yours truly." When I look back on my past behaviors, I really can't believe how untouchable I thought I was. Okay, so I'm being euphemistic. I know "stupid" is probably the description you had in mind.

I had to be invincible to survive all the hairy situations I put myself into. What else could I think? Well, it was several weeks after a diagnosis of Parkinson's Disease, and wouldn't you know it, I still thought I was invincible. Even though I felt that nothing could touch me, I did not pretend that my illness didn't exist, however. I did do my homework. I read up on the disease and discovered that some people have lived very well with Parkinson's. Since the disease affects everyone differently, I was certain that I would have the milder form of it. And in some cases, the disease can progress very slowly. Again, I took it for granted that I would belong to this elite group. So I had a reason to hope. However, I also discovered that younger patients—only five percent of Parkinsonians develop symptoms before the age of forty—tend to have a more variant form of the disease. Furthermore, side-effects from medications tend to be more severe in younger patients. To top it all off, most research studies excluded patients under age forty, because they are so rare, and their progression is so unpredictable. But this information conveniently floated over my head. After all, none of it could possibly apply to me. I remained sure that I was physically too strong to succumb to the same symptoms that plagued other Parkinsonians.

Strength or denial?

My air of invulnerability actually seemed to work for a while. Everybody that knew of my diagnosis marveled at how well I was coping with my fate. I would frequently hear, "I don't know how you do it," or "You are so strong." I didn't think I was being particularly strong at all. Given my warped sense of reality, I honestly thought it was no big deal. That's because like most people facing a loss of some kind, I was heavily entrenched in denial. I guess it was my mind's defense mechanism, to give me some time to assimilate all the ramifications of my illness. And in retrospect, I definitely did everything in my power to disassociate myself from Parkinson's Disease.

The "P" word

One of the red flags that signaled I was in denial was my refusal to say the word, "Parkinson's." I just couldn't do it. Instead, I would say, "my situation," or "my condition." And if anyone else happened to say that cursed word, I would visibly cringe. I even went so far as to tell people not to say the "P" word, as I called it. I guess I thought if I heard people say "Parkinson's," I might start believing I actually had it. And I just couldn't, or wouldn't, accept that. Denial was a safe place—for a little while.

Chapter Two

Impossible To Ignore

With my symptoms in check, and my emotional state protected by denial, I did pretty well during the following year. I was playing a lot of tennis and basketball without too much problem. I was frequently going out, gallivanting with my friends, as well. It was a fun year.

No More Grace Period

Then, just like that, the honeymoon was over. Practically overnight, I noticed a marked decline in my coordination, and I was constantly fatigued. It finally happened; I could no longer deny my fate. Sure, since the very onset of my symptoms, I had problems with my fine motor skills, making tasks such as fastening small buttons very problematic. But now, my athletic ability, the very source of my self-esteem, was being usurped from me. My endurance and coordination were so compromised, I was being dominated in basketball by aging weekend warriors at the club where I worked. My body just wasn't doing what I wanted it to do. It was so frustrating losing to guys that two years earlier, I would have beaten blindfolded.

I know I sound like a sore loser, but honestly, losing a silly game never bothered me before. No, this was something entirely different. To me, losing in such a pathetic fashion signified losing my ability to function. The icing on the cake was getting instructions on how to play basketball from the peanut gallery. I am speaking about pearls of wisdom such as: "You need to box out!" or "Come on, hustle! I thought you were supposed to be a personal trainer!" My only recourse was to keep quiet, and swallow my pride, despite wanting to explode with excuses for my ineptitude. But I couldn't allow myself the luxury of venting. My illness was a private matter, and I wanted to keep it that way.

Losing my physical prowess was a hard pill to swallow. I could no longer pride myself on my dazzling athletic skills. Instead, I had to live in the past. I felt like a repressed Al Bundy, from *Married with Children*. Every time I would do something klutzy in an athletic setting, I pictured Al with his hand in his pants, muttering, "When I played high school football, I scored four touchdowns in one game." From every roof top, I wanted to shout out all the things I *used to* be able to do. But unlike Bundy, I kept my glory days to myself. And it was frustrating.

It seemed like I was living in the past when it came to everything. No matter what I was talking about, or even thinking of, my illness was always a reference point. If I was talking about a past event with someone, I would mentally reference it as pre-Parkinson's or post-Parkinson's. For instance, I would think to myself, "Oh, that was two years pre-Parkinson's, when my body still functioned." I even stopped looking at old photos of myself, because I couldn't help pining for my pre-Parkinson's days. For those dealing with the loss of health or a loved one, living in the past is common because the future is so hard to face.

No Relief

I was certainly discouraged, especially since it seemed that I was deteriorating too rapidly. So I went back to the doctor for some answers. Over the next several months, he put me on many different drugs, none of which worked at all. That is not to say they did not have an effect. One of them left quite an impression as a matter of fact.

I took my first pill around 8PM, and wound up going to sleep two hours later. That's 10PM for those of you keeping score. At about midnight, a terrible feeling—akin to being stung by a swarm of bees—abruptly awakened me. When I sat up, I was confounded by hallucinations. I would imagine it was something similar to a bad LSD trip. I got up and tried to walk downstairs, where my girlfriend was watching television. But the room was spinning so badly, that I barely made it to the bottom step before I blacked out. A few seconds later, while my girlfriend was trying to bring me back to reality, I greeted her with a re-creation from the Exorcist. No, not the head spinning; the projectile vomiting. For an hour, I sat there with my body trembling uncontrollably. Then, I vomited a second time. Anyway, you get the picture—it was a long night.

The Worst of a Bad Situation

Since my symptoms were quickly getting worse, and I was not responding to any medications, except the first one, the doctor started questioning the diagnosis. You see, most people who are diagnosed with Parkinson's Disease have typical/idiopathic variety. You know, run-of-the-mill type stuff. But on occasion, what is first thought to be typical Parkinson's, turns out to be something different—something worse.

It was explained to me that I might have one or more, of many variant forms of the disease, including Shy-Drager Syndrome, Striatonigral Degeneration, and Olivopontocerebellar Atrophy. If they don't sound too good, it's because they're not. The implications of these diseases are more dire than regular PD, and their symptoms are virtually impossible to treat. Clinically speaking, however, I didn't completely fit the profile for any of these conditions.

My last option was to try the most effective Parkinson's drug—levodopa. Usually, this drug is held off until absolutely necessary, because of potentially serious side effects. But apparently, my response to it, or lack thereof, would be a strong indicator of which disease I actually had. So, optimistically, I started on the levodopa. The drug's main side effects, such as dyskinesias—unwanted wiggly movements—usually occur a few years after starting on it. "Usually" being the operative word. I suppose I'm unusual, because I had side effects from day one, including dyskinesias and extreme nausea. Just for good measure, the drug caused painful dystonia—cramping—in my left hand and foot. Not only did this make walking very painful, but it turned my hand into a permanent claw. Unfortunately, on top of all the side effects, there was minimum symptom relief.

So there I was, back at the doctor's office again, pleading for answers. None were to be had. He was as confused as

I was, and frankly, to his credit, he did not hide that fact. There was good news, however. I learned of one fool-proof way to get a definite diagnosis. The bad news was that it was by way of an autopsy. I told the doctor that I wasn't quite that anxious for a diagnosis after all.

Basically, my only option was to try to deal with my symptoms as best as I could, and wait it out. Supposedly, the speed and the form of the disease's progression would eventually lead to a more solid diagnosis. At least that was the hope. Ask anyone who is waiting on a firm diagnosis for any illness. The uncertainty is tortuously difficult. One of my only comforts had been knowing exactly what I was up against. Now, I didn't even have that. The result was terrible fear and anxiety, the likes of which I had never experienced before. For the first time in my life, I felt completely vulnerable.

CHAPTER THREE

Illness Can Destroy More Than The Body

If we lived in a vacuum, many of our hardships would be easier to cope with. But, as you know, we don't. So when a serious illness comes crashing into your life, unfortunately, you can't drop everything in order to deal with it. Bills still have to be paid, relationships still have to be nurtured, and responsibilities still have to be fulfilled. But as my disease consumed more and more of my attention, the other aspects of my life suffered commensurately. Picture this. If my life was the water filled to the top of a bucket, and Parkinson's was a cinder block being immersed in it, what would happen? Something has to give.

My deteriorating condition, coupled with the anxiety of an uncertain diagnosis, was definitely taking its toll. But I elected to hide my inner turmoil from everyone around me, pretending that I didn't have a care in the world. Furthermore, whenever I neglected a responsibility, I would pretend to be nonchalant, instead of admitting I was overwhelmed. But the burden kept mounting, and I was using all my resources to deal with it. Unfortunately, this left me without the mental energy to concentrate on anything else in my life. And to my dismay, there would eventually be a great price to pay.

Growing Pains

Trying to become acclimated to the fact that your body is slowly failing takes time. This adjustment period is often a bumpy ride, full of surprises and snafus. Well, once my symptoms became blatantly obvious, my family and friends needed time to adjust to my "new life," as well. It was not an easy process. Getting through the growing pains was just another challenge Parkinson's Disease was imposing on me and my loved ones.

For instance, one particular afternoon, my father and I were barricading my apartment in preparation for a potential hurricane. One of the tasks at hand was to tape some tarpaulin onto the outside of my kitchen window. However, I lacked the dexterity to hold the tarp with one hand, and tear pieces of tape off with the other. As I was struggling to attempt this great feat, my father said, in a huff, "Tony, come on. What are you doing?" Evidently, he thought I was futzing around.

Of course, I didn't blame him for his impatience. After all, at that point in time, he was unaware of exactly what I could, and could not do. My motor skills were abandoning me so swiftly, that even I was ignorant to the full extent of my limitations. But being scolded for my disability was terribly frustrating, nonetheless. Every similar encounter increased my frustration, and created undue tension in my interpersonal relationships.

My loved ones were forced to learn, on the fly, what my limitations were. But they also struggled to find the appropriate way to interact, in general, with a recently sentenced "sick" person. And like in any crisis situation, different individuals will each have their own special way of dealing with the "victim." Unfortunately, having a serious illness tends to elicit exaggerated responses from others.

Some people handled me with kid gloves, treating me like a sick puppy, and speaking to me extra softly. Maybe they thought I would break or something. Frankly, as much as I appreciated the sentiment, it became very irritating. That was one extreme. At the other extreme were those who didn't want to baby me, so they took the "drill sergeant" approach. They hoped that encouraging words might "motivate" my symptoms away. "You could move faster if you really tried," and "You can do it, you're just being lazy," were among the greatest hits. And again, as much as I tried to acknowledge their good intentions, I couldn't help feeling resentful for what I perceived to be their insensitivity.

Work

Fatigue was really starting to be problematic, especially at work. Working long hours was wearing me out. Naturally, this made me less enthused about doing my job, which hampered my ability to motivate clients. And as a personal trainer, being able to motivate your clients is not only important, it's everything. I had no energy to exercise myself, so my untrainer-like body wasn't too inspiring either. Feeling so wiped out all the time made me grumpy, as well. Also affecting my mood was the fact that my symptoms were starting to become apparent to people at the gym. I was not very comfortable with that. So I made excuses. I blamed my limp on a bum knee, which at least was half true. I did have a bad knee, but it didn't cause my limp. As far as my overall stiffness, I attributed it to a bad neck and back. That was certainly true. I simply omitted the little detail that Parkinson's was to blame for it. And as much as I tried to hide my trembling hand in my pants pocket, some people still noticed it. Only a few commented, however. I just pretended not to hear them.

A major dilemma for me was getting started in the morning. When I got out of bed, I was very stiff and slow for a good while. It took forever to get ready, especially if I needed to shave, or look for some clean clothes to wear. Things like simple hygiene had become major chores. Consequently, I was usually five or ten minutes late for my morning clients. Some clients were easy going, and let it slide. Others had a habit of reprimanding me and making a big fuss. All I could do was apologize profusely. I was learning rather quickly that humble pie for breakfast was not my favorite meal of the day.

I suppose I could've forced myself to get up thirty minutes earlier every day to prepare for contingencies, but I didn't. Sleep is a very precious commodity to the Parkinsonian. As it was, I felt like I needed double the sleep that I was actually getting. Cutting that amount even more would have magnified the severity of my symptoms to a point where I would've been totally useless. There was no recourse—my work-life was suffering.

Relationship

I would have been lucky if work had been the only casualty of my illness. No, Parkinson's is not that merciful.

Getting a neurological disease was not something I had ever bargained for. My girlfriend never bargained for it either. But it was foisted upon her just the same. The difference was: I had no way out, and she did. I have to hand it to her; she didn't bail out on me. Over the years, I have heard countless stories of people just picking up and deserting their spouses who have fallen ill. It's tragic, but all too common. Katie chose to hang in there, though. But our relationship was definitely taking a beating.

Even though I appeared to be coping well, in reality, my mind was a garbled mess. One contributing factor to the problem was my fear of running out of time. Time for what, you say? Everything and anything, I guess. I was trying to cram every ounce of fun I could into a rapidly closing window of opportunity. Therefore, I spent a lot of time pampering myself, going to sporting events, and hanging out with friends.

Unfortunately, I neglected my girlfriend in the process. Candidly, I took her for granted. I figured she would always be around, so why not be self-indulgent until my disability prevents me from doing so. A secondary reason for the neglect was that being home forced me to face my situation. Since my girlfriend knew I was ill, I couldn't hide from reality at home. She was the only one who was able to see all my frailties and vulnerabilities. Hanging out with my friends, on the other hand, was time filled with frivolity and superficiality. I didn't have to think about my illness, or the future, or anything at all. It was easier to defer my pain with diversions. I sought refuge in places where my fear and self-doubt weren't so transparent. Previously, I had been denying my fate. Now, I was running from it.

Something else that caused a rift in our relationship was our different philosophies, vis-à-vis my condition. I had one way of dealing with my illness, and she had another. And they did not jibe with each other. With what I was going through, my fragile ego yearned for some attention. I wanted some sort of acknowledgment or understanding of the burden I was carrying, and maybe a pat on the back every once in a while. That was not her approach. Instead, her view was that I should just accept things as they are, and move on. Although she did everything in her power to make my life easier, she refused to coddle me emotionally. I honestly don't think she understood that Parkinson's was eating away at more than just my body. Thus, I began to perceive her as insensitive, while at the same time, she perceived me as weak.

As you can see, our relationship faced many problems. But there were even more. Our relationship suffered further because I was extremely self-absorbed. My illness became an excuse for all my screw-ups. As in the time I didn't get her a Valentine's day gift. Not only did I fail to apologize, but I became indignant because she got upset. My attitude was that she should understand that I was too tired to go shopping for a gift. Of course, I was too tired to get her Christmas or birthday presents either. It was true; I was always exhausted. There was still no excuse.

Despite our problems, Katie and I were still hanging on by a thread. Talk of splitting up, however, was starting to become serious. Then one day, I heard a familiar chuckle in the distance. I could have sworn it came from the heavens. Yes, God was at it again.

New Baby

Her voice, much like my left hand, was very shaky. It was Katie calling me from work. She needed to tell me something. The trepidation in her voice put me on edge. I really started to panic when she asked, "Are you sitting down?" My stomach churned, anticipating the worst. When she told me that she was pregnant, I breathed a sigh of relief. Despite the troubles we were having, there was not a moment of hesitation on my part—I instantly, and inexplicably, felt a connection to my future child. She was relieved, but surprised as well.

She was surprised with good reason. For two years, she had heard me saying, ad nauseam, that I didn't want children. As a matter of fact, only a month or two earlier, we had discussed the issue again. And again, I was adamant about not having children, especially in light of my condition. "After all," I argued, "kids are a lot of responsibility, and if anything, I need to lighten my load." But my reaction to the news of her pregnancy was visceral, not intellectual. I couldn't explain it. I just knew that I wanted this child. Today, I know at least two things beyond the shadow of a doubt: Firstly, my son was, and is, a gift from God; and secondly, I was as wrong as any person can be about not wanting kids. In my heart, I know I was saved that day. The irony is, I was saved, in large part, from my own ignorance.

New Fears

The prospect of being new parents invigorated our relationship. Picking out names, imagining how our child would look, and the rest of the wonderful things associated with impending parenthood, brought us a lot of joy. But as the months passed, and I could actually feel the baby kick, reality set in. Well, my reality that is.

With each passing day, I became more anxious about my future. It was so uncertain, and in my eyes, not all that rosy. I was incredibly worried about my future as a father, and the future of my son.(I was convinced our child would be a boy.) Would I bring my son down with me? Would I even be able to play with him? Or teach him how to play baseball? Or go camping with him? And if I couldn't, who would? Would my son learn to love that person more than me? And when he starts playing little league, will he be embarrassed that his "shaky" dad is at the game? How much of a burden will I be on my family? For every fear a person could think of, I came up with two more. Being able to provide for my child financially also weighed heavily on my mind. I desperately tried to hide these fears from the people around me. But it was impossible. The fear began to manifest itself physically, in ways that were obvious, albeit bewildering, to others. The physical effect my anxiety was having on my body was frightening to say the least.

The fear I was toting around with me felt like a lead brick in my stomach. It was with me constantly. Then there would be times throughout the day when my heart would race uncontrollably. The heart pounding was accompanied by profuse sweating and shortness of breath. Most people would have thought they were having a heart attack, but I was lucky enough to realize that I was suffering from panic attacks. My friend had an anxiety disorder, so I was familiar with the symptoms. In fact, he once had an episode so severe that he actually went blind for about a minute. Believe me, having a panic attack is not simply a matter of being nervous. Despite what most people think, it can be quite debilitating. Thankfully, I never went blind, but sometimes these episodes were unbearable nonetheless. Consequently, my behavior was often a bit erratic.

Here's an example. One night around 11PM, Katie and I were watching television. We were watching a program which I was basically oblivious to, up until they showed a father and son restoring a classic car together. Nice enough content for the average bear. But for me, it was the start of an avalanche. A surge of fear swept over me like a sand storm. The rush of anxiety was indescribable, and inescapable. My head felt like it was going to implode, and my stomach was twisting in knots. All I wanted to do was run. I tried my hardest to explain to Katie that I needed to get some fresh air, but my mutterings were probably unintelligible. So I bolted out of the house in the middle of the night to go for a drive. Now how could I explain this odd behavior to her, when in truth, I didn't understand it myself? What could I have said, "It's the panic attacks that are to blame?" I would have had better luck saying, "The devil made me do it." Either way, she wasn't buying it.

The lack of understanding, on both our parts, was causing tension, resentment, and more anxiety. Our relationship continued to deteriorate throughout the remainder of the pregnancy. What should have been a happy time was instead a stressful one. And in her mind, it was my fault. Even though I could plead extenuating circumstances, for the most part, she was right.

Chapter Four
One Hardship Begets Another

The birth of our beautiful boy, Nicolas Anthony Scelta, offered us new hope. We could now share our love with our precious child, and perhaps find new incentive to make the relationship work. I'll never forget how he was ushered into this world—with his eyes wide open. From that moment, I was instantly smitten. I was such a proud daddy, and so completely in love with my little treasure. By this time, my panic attacks were virtually gone, but unfortunately, Mr.Fear was still lurking close by.

Fish Out of Water

Yes, the old fears were still part of the picture, but new ones had come to the forefront. Particularly, the fear of not being equipped to take care of a newborn. When Nico was only three days old, I realized I was out of my league. That's when my girlfriend went back to work, and left me alone to take care of him. She really had no choice. After all, it was quite apparent that I wasn't going to be the breadwinner of the household. So there I was, the proverbial fish out of water. I was responsible for the care of my son, despite never having held a baby before in my life. I was totally clueless.

Trust me, I realize that not all first-time dads are this helpless. My friend, Chris, for instance, was Superdad from day one. Maybe it was because of his experience as a Paramedic, dealing with all sorts of emergency situations. He is definitely a take control type of guy. On that particular day with Nico, I was anything but in control. Despite the baby being asleep most of the day, I was so nervous that I could hardly breathe. All I could think of was, "What if something happens—how will I know what to do?" "What if I *know* what to do, but I'm too slow and clumsy to actually *do* it?"

I was even more nervous when Nico was awake, which usually meant he was eating. It was very strange feeding my son for the first time. My heart was racing, but I was hanging in there, until he started choking on his formula. He was coughing so hard that his little face turned bright red. Not a grave ordeal for the average parent, right? Well to me, on that occasion, it was terribly frightening. Did I do something wrong? Was this normal? I was a nervous wreck. By the end of the day, I was seriously questioning my self-worth. Never before had I felt so useless.

I was thrown into the deep end of the pool on my third day of fatherhood. But Nico and I got through it. I presumed things could only get easier. Wouldn't you know it, I was wrong again? Something called Colic made sure of that. Anyone ever hear of it? It's the family version of Chinese Water Torture only worse. For those of you who have not had a colicky baby, thank your lucky stars. Ask any parent who has, and they'll tell you that it's a living hell. For at least five months, my son was constantly crying in agony.

I'm sure you can imagine how incredibly stressful having a colicky baby can be on a marriage or relationship. Not only is the experience emotionally draining, but it's physically draining as well from being kept awake all night. That combination could put anyone on edge. One time, when Katie was fifteen minutes late from work, I tore into her because I had to go to work myself. The fifteen extra minutes of hearing my son cry pushed me right over the edge. As I got in my car, I nearly broke down from frustration. Katie and I found ourselves wanting to get away from each other, more and more frequently. That is until one day, she decided to get away....for good.

Single Dad

She finally had enough. When Nico was ten months old, my girlfriend moved out of the house. The idea was, if our relationship was not going to work, it was better to split up before Nico would be old enough to know the difference. It made sense, I guess. If we were to break up when he was three or four years old, he would be devastated. So following our hearts, we did what we thought was best for our child. We decided that I should take care of him during the day, and that she would have him at night. We each had an entire day with him on the weekends. This was the best way we knew how to make the transition easiest for Nico. As it turns out, I was the one most traumatized.

As I sat in my bedroom that first night, alone, with my son's crib empty, I contemplated taking drugs for the first time in my life. The pain was so intense. I couldn't conceive of things getting any better either. Ruminations over the sheer gravity of my predicament engulfed my mind. How would I survive? I was barely working because of my condition, and also because of the time I was dedicating to Nico. So there was no way I could afford the rent. And my condition was getting worse. I was so tired all the time that I didn't even have the energy to feed myself. But my most pressing concern was: Who would help me take care of Nico when my illness became untenable? I stayed up all night, toiling. I was in the midst of something very foreign to me—a deep depression.

Over the next several weeks I lost twenty-five pounds. Even though I stood six feet tall, I managed to drop down to a sickly 145 pounds. My friends literally thought I was at death's door. I had to assure everyone that I was in good health, other than the Parkinson's of course. My days were agonizing and somber. I was hopeless. Although I have always been staunchly against the use of mind-altering substances, there were several instances when I considered taking drugs to numb the pain. I have to admit, the only thing that stopped me was my son. I knew he deserved better than that. I needed to take care of him, and I couldn't afford to handicap myself any further. My only glimmer of hope was that the storm would somehow subside to a point where I could at least function.

And eventually it did. After a few weeks, the intense pain had abated to a bearable level. My outlook on the future was still bleak, and I was still fraught with anxiety, but I was no longer in the abyss. Since I couldn't afford my rent, my brother took me into his home. Even though I felt like a burden, it was a relief to have a place to stay. Soon after moving in with him, I stopped working all together. I'm not certain if it was the stress or not, but my symptoms were considerably worse than ever before. I was moving in slow motion, and I was exhausted twenty-four hours a day. Thank God for my brother—at least my son and I had a roof over our heads. He even went the extra mile and fed us once in a while.

It was quite a whirlwind ride, those two years after Katie got pregnant. I went from a self-sufficient maverick, who didn't want kids, to being the disabled, destitute, single dad of a baby boy. But the ride had only just begun. I was all on my own with Nico now. I think most people would agree that being a single mother is difficult. Many would argue that being a single father, with no maternal instincts, might be a tad more challenging. Well, a single father with Parkinson's has much heavier challenges to contend with. Everyday aspects of parenthood were so laborious for me, that in retrospect, it was downright comical. I could probably even write an entire book on my misadventures.

The follies of a single dad with Parkinson's

Where should I begin? Well, I'll backtrack a little, and start with an incident that happened before Katie and I separated. When Nico was about five months old, I took him to a friend's house. It was the first time that I had taken him somewhere in the car by myself. The truth is, my fine motor skills were so deficient, that I didn't feel confident venturing out alone with the baby. Nice walks with him in the stroller were the extent of our outings together. But this time, I decided to be brave. So I put him in the car, struggled a little to get him in the car seat, and off we went.

Twenty minutes later, we arrived at our destination. My friend was waiting outside, and promptly removed Nico from his seat before I could get out of the car. Once we were inside the house, my son was having a pleasant time, despite still being a bit colicky. But for me, it was just another stressful event. Within minutes of arriving, I was anxious to get back to the comforts of home base, where I could control my environment. Needless to say, our stay was brief.

On the way home, Nico started crying in pain. I couldn't wait to get home. As soon as we got there, I attempted to get him out of the car seat. The only glitch was that my fingers refused to cooperate. So with Nico wailing in my ear, I desperately fought with this contraption. As the minutes passed, and the sweat poured off me in the hot Florida sun, a tempest raged in my gut. That inner voice we all have was screaming, "How could I be this helpless? Is it asking too much to be able to remove my crying child from his car seat?" Evidently, it was. Luckily I composed myself and called a nearby friend for assistance.

Looking back on that day, I laugh at what a clown I must have looked like. But back then it was no laughing matter. It was quite the opposite, in fact. You see, the rage within me didn't just disappear—it festered. Each similar incident was like an assault on my self-esteem, as well as on my overall psyche. And the damage was adding up.

Changing diapers. Boy, I sure don't miss that. Not because of the smell, mind you. No, I had that covered. Parkinson's ruined my sense of smell even before Nico was born. So I was pretty much immune. Who said Parkinson's was all bad? It actually comes in handy some times. Unfortunately, my illness made the process of changing diapers much more adventurous than I would have preferred.

I want you to indulge me for a second. Picture yourself

trying to change a baby's diaper. This particular baby hates being changed, and consequently squirms and kicks with a vengeance. Now imagine that your left arm is so uncoordinated that it was practically useless. Keep in mind, also, that the fingers on my right hand weren't exactly adroit, either. Can you picture the scene? Are you appreciating the frustration? No need for alarm folks, this is just a drill. Unfortunately, this exercise in futility was not make-believe for me. When Katie and I were still together, I tried to limit this frustrating activity as much as possible. And after we split up? Well, let's just say I was in a state of perpetual frustration.

Let me tell you, the fun never ends when you're a spaz. One particular evening, at a nice Italian restaurant, I was on a first date with a completely enthralling woman. My son was with us, because I never left him with anybody else on our scheduled nights together. Besides, my date actually suggested that I bring him. The place was nice and cozy, and the conversation was going smoothly. But right after we ordered our food, I detected a foul stench emanating from my son's direction. Now since I had a compromised sense of smell, my date must have been appreciating the aroma for quite some time. I was not a happy camper. Changing diapers at home was difficult enough. But to pull it off in the men's restroom would take some divine intervention. With no other choice, I scurried off to give it a try.

What happened next is a testament to the fact that when you think things can't possibly get worse, you should think again. Nico happened to be wearing overalls with two iron clasps on them. As hard as I tried, they wouldn't budge. That voice inside was yelling again, "Arrggghhh! I told her (his mother) ten times not to dress him in overalls when I pick him up!" The only solution I could think of was to cut the straps off. So I nonchalantly walked back into the dining area, scooped up a knife from one of the tables, and retreated. I felt like a complete loon. Back in the bathroom, I frantically started cutting, while Nico was dangling in the air. It was a scene out of a Jim Carrey movie. *Dumb and Dumber* is the one that comes to mind. By the time the cutting and changing debacle was finally over, my dinner companion had already finished her meal. As for me? I looked like I had just gone through a car wash—without my car. There is no doubt; I have had cooler moments.

Losing Friends

As we get older, it becomes harder to maintain solid friendships. People are busy with the demands of work and family, and have little time to devote to many other things. Throw an illness into the mix, or any hardship for that matter, and it becomes that much more difficult. When you have Parkinson's, it's almost impossible to be reliable. I can't even count how many times I made plans with a friend, but had to cancel because I didn't feel well. People eventually start to get tired of it. Especially if they don't grasp exactly what you're going through. And few people ever really do. They figure if you're not in a wheelchair, and you can still speak, you must be fine. It can be very dispiriting to feel so horrible inside, and hear remarks like, "What could you possibly be tired from? You did nothing all day." The fact is, it always took a great effort to appear even somewhat normal in public. Furthermore, I only came out of hiding when I was at my best. The rest of the time, I remained a recluse. And even from home, I would sometimes be too tired to simply return a phone call. It's hard to keep friends that way. There was just no way they could understand.

This lack of understanding not only resulted in friends writing me off, but the opposite as well. Insensitive things people would say really bothered me. Whenever one friend in particular would have a "rough" day at work, she would say with an attitude, "Well, *some* of us have to work." Sure, ignorance, and not malice, was predominantly at the root of the problem, but it was still hard not to take it personally. I even responded one time with, "Hey, anytime you want to switch places....." Unfortunately, it didn't sink in. Another condescending remark that I heard from a few people was, "Look at Janet Reno—she's got Parkinson's, and she is doing fine." I welcomed this comment as much as a smoker, dying of lung cancer, would welcome, "What's *your* problem? So-and-so has been smoking for fifty years and he is just fine." As a result of how certain individuals made me feel, I gradually distanced myself from them. Fortunately for me, I had a few friends that were, and always have been, very understanding and supportive. They are true blue.

Dating

I'm going to go out on a limb, and say that one of the most important things in life, for many of us, is to meet the person of our dreams, and fall in love. Well, as you can imagine, having Parkinson's Disease made meeting people rather challenging. Most Parkinsonians are much older, and already have spouses that hopefully love them and take care of them. So they're fortunate, at least from that aspect. I, however, was back to square one; back on the market. I wasn't too enthused about that fact either. For some outlandish reason, I thought being penniless, disabled, and depressed, might affect my market value. Crazy, huh?

Since I had no intentions of becoming a monk, I started dating, despite my pessimism. My foray onto the social scene was incredibly nerve-racking, even when Nico wasn't pooping in his pants in front of my dates. In the past, I was very confident and self-assured in this area. Perhaps I was no Casanova, but I think I held my own in the charm department. But in the post-Parkinson's era, any sign of charm was glaringly absent. Mr.Cool was long gone. His replacement was an insecure man, riddled with anxiety, and trying to hide his frailties.

Of course they were impossible to hide, especially since stress exacerbates the symptoms of my condition. A new symptom that I was graced with at the time—dermatitis—was also impossible to hide. It was like having a bad case of dandruff that is not happy being relegated to the scalp. My head and face felt like one big, red, itchy flake. Eventually, I found a medication to control it, but only after the requisite number of lessons in humility. I felt so undesirable that I was amazed when a woman actually wanted to see me again. It must have been my secret weapon. But anyhow, that's classified information.

Every date that I had presented its own challenges. Certain choices always had to be made. If the date was at a restaurant, I would only order finger foods, because I had trouble handling a fork and knife. If it was at a bar or club, I had to be able to sit down, so my back would not cramp up. And if the setting was more intimate, I had a personal choice to make. Take it easy, it's not what you think. I had to consider whether or not to have a glass of wine to relax my nerves. This would minimize my tremor, but aggravate my problems with coordination and slowness of movement. But without the wine, I tended to shy away from physical contact for fear of shaking out of my socks. It can be quite distracting trying to kiss someone while your body's scoring an 8.5 on the Richter scale. Ahh, decisions, decisions.

On one occasion, I was invited to someone's house for dinner: The whole family of five and me, Mr.Gregarious. Ordinarily, I would have declined, because those types of situations made me feel exposed, and very nervous. But in this case, I had known the girl for a few weeks, and had previously met her family. So, being a glutton for punishment, I accepted. We had spaghetti and meatballs, which was an auspicious start to the evening. Not just because I'm Italian, but because this was a meal that I wouldn't have to wrestle with to eat. But half way through supper, I started to feel nauseated. A new medication I was taking was attempting to ruin my night. I tried to ride out the storm, but a perspiration shower and a pale face gave me away. I was forced to excuse myself, and lie down. Everyone always wants to make a good impression on the family of the person they're dating. This was not the impression that I had in mind.

While embarrassing moments like this had an effect on my self-esteem, they did not scare me away from women. I guess pride has nothing on the power of hormones. What us poor saps will go through for a woman's affections! Honestly though, hormones had little to do with my desire to meet someone. It's been said that, "Behind every great man, there is a great woman." Well, I had no one by my side. I had no one to lift my spirits when I was feeling low. There was no special lady in my life to support me, love me, and make me strong. Nor was there anyone to share special times with. Damn, I have to stop—I'm depressing myself. My point is, at a time when I desperately needed all the help I could get, some companionship would have helped a great deal.

That's why I continued to date, no matter how uncomfortable it was. Usually, I endured the most grief within the first few dates. After my condition was out on the table, and the person knew what to expect, I relaxed a bit. And sometimes, not.

I remember when I had dinner with a person who already knew of my condition. She actually read up on Parkinson's before our date. What she didn't read, however, was that people with my condition often display a "poker face." Because the facial muscles are rigid and uncoordinated, the Parkinsonian's face is often expressionless. So whenever I looked at her that night, she would say, "Why are you staring at me?" Since it was embarrassing to blame everything on my illness, I said something corny like, "It's because you're so beautiful." The poker face also made me appear grumpy or angry, when in fact, I wasn't. It's hard to convince someone that you're not grumpy, when your lifeless mug is telling them otherwise. And you know the saying: Those that laugh, laugh together, but those that frown, frown alone. Isn't that how it goes? Well, if not, I'm hoping you'll let me slide on this one.

Chapter Five

Fading Fast

Although I am trying to make light of all my silly escapades, and my wrestling matches with articles of clothing, in truth, I was in serious trouble. I basically saw my life as over. The only reason I continued to get up every morning was my son. I knew that I still could offer him many things, especially all my love. But the hope for me was gone. I viewed my situation from the perspective of a death row inmate—I was counting the days before the inevitable. I believed the inevitable ending that loomed for me was total debilitation. Before this point, I still held on to a morsel of hope; the possibility of a "stay of execution" that only medical science could provide. In my mind, the only thing that could rescue me was a legitimate cure for Parkinson's disease. But after struggling for so long, without any progress towards a cure, I had given up on science too.

When I first got diagnosed, there seemed to be a lot of excitement about the future treatments of brain disease. I figured it was only a matter of time. What I didn't realize is that science moves at its own pace. Trying to find an effective drug or treatment, for any disease, is a long and arduous process.

Not to mention of course, it takes money—lots of it. By the time a pharmaceutical company even gets to test a drug on humans, they've invested tens of millions of dollars already. After many more millions, and five or six more years, it might reach the consumer. The sad part is, at the end of the day, most of these drugs are disappointments. Over the years, since my diagnosis, there were a few huge disappointments with respect to treatments for Parkinson's. There was so much hype and promise regarding several different drugs, with no results. Each time that I was disappointed, the modicum of hope I did have left, diminished further, until there was none left at all.

I Can't Deal with This Anymore

No one should ever lose hope. Hopelessness is a dangerous and scary state to be in. Illness can do that to a person. I had all but given up, which was something I thought would never happen. This scourge called Parkinson's had dismantled my life. It was an unstoppable force, and I didn't know how much more I could take.

Chemical saboteur

I was surely scraping the bottom of the abyss. If only I could find the motivation to climb out. If only I could feel good about something. I just couldn't. Well, it turns out that I had more against me then I realized. Get ready for the coup de grace. The neurotransmitter in our brains responsible for producing feelings of satisfaction, pleasure, and motivation, is called dopamine. The brain cells that are dying in the Parkinsonian's brain produce—you guessed it—dopamine. No wonder I couldn't pull myself out of the quagmire—I was being burned at both ends!

Chemical imbalances in the brain are not to be trivialized. People with ostensibly great lives can become virtually catatonic due to a lack of a certain neurotransmitter, such as serotonin for example. People such as this can stay depressed for years, mired in a state of hopelessness, all because of one little chemical in the brain.

As for my favorite chemical, even slightly less than optimum levels of dopamine in the brain has been associated with depression, as well as with drug and alcohol addiction. Addicts use these substances because they induce feelings of gratification and pleasure. How do these drugs do that? Predominantly, by increasing dopamine levels in the brain. This dopamine dilemma means that people with Parkinson's face a unique challenge. If their physical ailments don't make them depressed, then the lack of pleasure-dependent dopamine in their brains probably will—twenty percent of Parkinsonians exhibit signs of severe depression even before the onset of any physical symptoms.

I may not have known that my disease was chemically sabotaging my happiness from the outset, but one thing I knew for certain—I desperately needed help. But I didn't know where to turn. It seemed that nothing could bring me out of my depressed state. My body was surely not giving me any reason to hope. And as we now know, my brain wasn't helping much either.

The stranger in the mirror

Feeling tired and sick all the time was bad enough. But when I looked in the mirror, or at a photograph, I felt even sicker. It was, somehow, confirmation that I was ill. I would see a picture of myself and think, "That's not me. It can't be." I didn't want to believe that this person, whom I did not recognize, was actually me. It was disheartening to constantly think, "That guy in the picture is not the stud-muffin I always knew and loved!" There was no way I could even rationalize the discrepancy. After all, pictures are only supposed to add pounds, not decades.

Physical suffering

Many people are under the misconception that Parkinson's just involves "the shakes." It's obviously much more than that. The symptoms of slowness, rigidity, lack of coordination, and tremor are always mentioned with regard to the subject of this disease. That's because these symptoms are visible to everyone. What most people don't realize is that this condition can also be extremely painful. For me, neck and back pain were a serious problem. I always tried to hide that aspect of the disease from everyone, but I know sometimes the anguish on my face gave me away. Unless of course, people just thought I had gas.

As bad as my pain was, others had it worse. I learned of a fellow Parkinsonian, who asked his doctor if it was possible to cut out part of his back muscles. Pain killers and muscle relaxers didn't help, so he was willing to do anything to find relief. Could you imagine the suffering it would take for someone to contemplate something so drastic?

Pain was not the only cause of my suffering. I was also dealing with debilitating fatigue. Even though I had been plagued by fatigue from almost the very beginning, it had gotten substantially worse. There had been a time when I could actually accomplish a few things, despite being exhausted. But six years into the disease, and I barely could do anything.

It was literally exhausting for me to do little things, like take a shower, or make myself a sandwich. Usually, I would flip a coin: Heads I'm stinking, tails I'm starving.

Live or Die

Everyone has their breaking point. I had finally reached mine. Despair had pushed me to the edge. After weeping for three or four days straight, I realized I had to do something. I had to pick a side. In the *Karate Kid,* the teacher, Mr. Myagi, spoke to his student about the importance of being committed to one side: "If there is a road, and you stand on one side of it, you will be safe. If you stand on the other side of the road, you also will be safe. But if you stand in the middle, you will get squashed, just like a grape." He continued to say that the same principle applies to karate. If you train half-heartedly, you will get squashed just like a grape. Waffling in the middle of the road, with no real goal, can be a precarious place to be in life as well. That's exactly where I was in my life; standing idly in the middle of the road, letting Parkinson's run me over like a Mack truck. I had to put an end to it once at for all. There was just no way that I could endure the punishment of being in the middle any longer. But which way would I go? Words from the movie, the *Shawshank Redemption*, described my choices perfectly. I could either, "get busy living, or get busy dying." Anywhere in between was pure hell.

God knows, I did not want to die. So at the proverbial moment of truth, I saw the correct path with absolute clarity. In fact, there had never been any other viable alternative. I needed to take my life back.

Enlightenment

I realized that I couldn't rely on a Parkinson's cure to save me, nor could I depend on anything, or anyone else, to do so either. I knew that I, and I alone, could save myself. But how? How could I rebuild my self-esteem and stave off depression? My life's passion—exercise—would have been the perfect panacea, if only I was healthy enough to do it. I wanted to workout so desperately, but my body wouldn't let me.

I started doing a lot of soul searching, and frankly, I began to feel like a hypocrite. I had always preached to my clients that exercise was the cure-all to pretty much all that ails us. But when things got tough for me, I abandoned something I really believed in. Sure, just walking around the block made my legs feel so weak and shaky that I would nearly vomit, but that was no excuse not to fight through it.

So I decided to force myself to do a few pushups. I managed to muster up the will-power to do about ten push-ups, but that one set took a lot out of me. Nonetheless, I psyched myself up to do another set of nine or ten. I should have stopped there. I didn't. During the third set, my body went limp and I fell to the floor. It must have been twenty minutes later when my brother walked in the front door and found me face down on his living room floor—I couldn't move.

This was not an auspicious kick-off to my fitness comeback tour. I realized that getting "psyched" to exercise was not going to be enough to overcome the physical limitations facing me. What I needed was a game plan.

Part II:

F.I.T. To Get Fit

Chapter Six
Building The Foundation

I found myself in a classic Catch 22 situation. In order to feel better mentally and emotionally, I needed my old reliable—exercise. But in order to find the will and the motivation to exercise, I needed to be strong, mentally and emotionally. So my only option was to get busy fortifying my mind, as well as my body.

I started out by trying to figure out exactly what makes certain people virtually undaunted by adversity. How do they persevere through pain and hardship, while the rest of us fret over things like a bad-hair-day? I decided to read countless stories of "beating the odds" to look for common denominators.

Then, after devouring dozens of books ranging from the self-help genre, to philosophy, I came to a few conclusions. In my analysis, there are three major commonalities shared by those that triumph in the face of extreme adversity. Most important among them is faith. Those who consistently overcome great hardships never doubt that they will achieve their goal. Secondly, there must be an adequate reason to persevere. In other words, they must be inspired to achieve their goal. Lastly, to get through difficult circumstances, one must never give up. Tenacity allows us to carry on through the toughest situations.

This little theory of mine seemed to ring true in every situation I could think of. To test it, I wanted to apply my F.I.T. theory (Faith, Inspiration, Tenacity) to an event in which I personally overcame an obstacle. Powerlifting immediately came to mind. So, as an example, I analyzed the mindset I employed when I used to perform the bench press.

The Building Blocks

As I approached the weight on the bench press, first and foremost in my mind was: I truly believed that I could perform the lift. I couldn't even imagine failing. If a smidgen of doubt entered my head, at any point, that weight would have crashed down on my chest like a ton of bricks. For me to succeed, I had to have *faith.*

Okay, so I believed that I could do it. The next question became, why should I do it? To the powerlifter, increased self-esteem, and a sense of achievement and power are ample reasons. These reasons were my *inspiration* to perform the task at hand.

Meanwhile, the 350 pound obstacle still stood in the way. Performing maximum lifts, such as I am describing, is extremely grueling, so *tenacity* is essential to completing the task. Often, while performing the bench press, the weight creeps upward very slowly. Sometimes, it even stops and sinks slightly downward. Any let up of effort, even for an instant, and it's all over. This is the point when you have to dig deep, and muster up more intensity than ever before.

Not Just Words

So now we know that faith, inspiration, and tenacity are necessary for defying despair? Is that realization enough to help anyone in despair? I doubt it. These words need meaning; they need context. The following few chapters provide that context by examining my experience, along with the experiences of many others who also have triumphed over despair.

Chapter Seven
Faith

Elusive Concept

My strategy for fighting despair started with the premise that we must truly believe we can overcome our particular hardships. This requires faith. But the concept of faith can be elusive. By itself, it may only have superficial meaning. For instance, if you tell someone who is despondent, "Don't worry, just have faith," you haven't given them much to grasp. In order for the concept to be useful, there has to be a solid basis behind it. My first endeavor was to examine all the elements that form this basis. The next step was to try to understand the process by which a person utilizes their faith to overcome grief. And finally, I wanted to know where the people without faith fit in. Can a person just magically make themselves believe in something? Furthermore, how can people, who are naturally negative and skeptical, overcome their predilections for doubt and disbelief?

Don't Be Afraid To Acquire a Little Knowledge

Socrates said, "Truly courageous action depends also on knowledge or wisdom, so that the action will be right." Well, based upon my limited personal experience, *every* action depends on knowledge. Therefore, to solve any problem, one must first seek out the truth. Skeptical people usually eschew ideas that they dislike, and gravitate towards things that they're more comfortable with. I know because I was one of them. Anything I couldn't see, touch, or grasp, wasn't real to me. I always considered myself to be an intelligent person, and maybe that was part of the problem. When you think you know it all, why bother listening to anything else?

Well, after I immersed myself in different philosophies, new and old, everything changed for me. That's not to say, however, that I necessarily bought into everything I read. On the contrary, I simply drew on the information so that I could form my own ideas. For me personally, the best way to formulate ideas, or to come to certain conclusions, is to ask the appropriate probing questions.

With regard to faith, the burning question for me was: Where does it stem from? My hope was that if I knew where faith came from, I could learn how to develop it. I concluded that people who overcome great adversity have a strong faith in God, and/or a strong faith in their own capabilities. My view is that the more you examine your faith, through learning and introspection, the stronger it will become. It follows then, that the stronger your faith is, the more successful your fight against despair will be.

Starting from Scratch

It might be difficult to examine your faith if you don't have any to begin with. In my case, I wasn't totally devoid of faith, but I didn't have much. During the time that I was in the midst of despair, I did believe in God, but had no faith that He could or would help me. Did I have faith in myself, at least? Nada. Zilch. Zero. Therefore, I had to learn how to develop my faith. So before we delve into specifics on having faith in God and having faith in yourself, let's lay some groundwork. Here are some ways that may help you to develop, or further develop your faith in general.

Observe, listen, and assimilate

I never realized how much I could learn from simply conversing with ordinary people. The key is to open up your heart to those around you. In return, they will open up to you about their experiences and feelings, both of which can offer you valuable insights.

Seek out positive people, particularly those who face adversity with a stiff chin and a smile. Discuss their faith with them and ask why they believe what they believe. You will discover that those with faith in God and/or themselves have much stronger convictions than those with no faith. In fact, those without faith usually have no convictions at all. Examine how each individual is living his or her life. Who are the ones that tend to be happier, stronger, and more positive? Who are the people that move you?

I think that if you make an honest effort to open up to other people's experiences, you will be able to develop, sustain, and fortify your faith. At the very least, you will become much wiser.

Just feel

For many people, faith is something that comes naturally. For them, it is a feeling that requires no searching, no effort, no introspection, and no nurturing. These fortunate folks seem to have an inherent belief that everything is as it should be. Invariably, they listen to their hearts above all else. We can learn from their example. Sometimes, it is necessary to put everything we know aside, tune out the noise that constantly inundates our brains, and just feel.

If you don't know what I mean, well.........you're in trouble. Don't fret though—you've come to the right place. Immersing yourself in nature is a good place to start. The next opportunity you get, I want you to get out of bed early, sit comfortably outside in silence, and watch the sun come up. Try to involve all your senses. Listen to the birds chirping. Feel the wind blowing against your skin. Smell the budding flowers or the freshly cut grass. Clear your mind completely and try to appreciate the marvel and wonderment of nature. Allow your heart to provide you with the answers that your brain simply cannot. In other words, the answers will not suddenly come into your head in the form of words such as: "Hello, this is God speaking." Nature, God, faith, and even love all defy description. The only way to truly know these concepts is to experience them. Simply appreciate your moment alone with nature and perhaps you will start to "feel" that everything is right in the world.

Faith in God

For all the non-believers reading this book, please don't skip ahead. Humor me for a few moments. It's not my goal to convert anyone. I do, however, want to convey the importance of hearing other viewpoints. Many times, listening to ideas contrary to yours, helps crystallize your own views even further. Then of course, there are those rare occasions when you actually modify your beliefs. Again, I am talking from experience, because I used to be an Agnostic. An Agnostic basically takes a "who knows" stance, neither believing in the existence of God, nor denying the existence of God.

Although I now believe and trust in God, this conversion was definitely a slow process. Incidentally, the process had nothing to do with my illness. This was not a situation in which I was desperate, and consequently turned to the nearest fantasy for help. Instead, my faith was borne out of something pure and good. My transformation started in a hospital room on May 3rd, 1998—the day my son was born. I guess you can say that when my son was born, my faith was born. Now, five years later, here I am—a believer.

Yes, it's hard to admit you were wrong. I'll say it, "I was wrong!" Wow! That was therapeutic. You have to give it a try sometime. But admitting it is not enough. It's more important to me that I discovered why I was wrong. And trust me, there were plenty of reasons.

Pain that runs deep

The first time I doubted the existence of God, I was in seventh grade. I went to a Catholic school in Queens, New York, where people took their little league baseball seriously. I was a baseball fanatic, and a very skilled player for my age. The previous year, when I was in sixth grade, I played on the school's seventh grade team—the first time the school had allowed that to happen, according to the coach.

Despite being younger than everyone else on the team, I was clearly the best player. I prayed every night to win the MVP trophy, which was to be presented at the end of the season. But right before the awards ceremony, the coach approached me with the bad news. He assured me that I deserved the MVP, but he could not give it to me. You see, it was a seventh grade team, and if a lowly sixth grader got the award, many people would be upset. I assumed he was referring to the parents of my teammates. The coach said that the next year would be different. I took this injustice pretty hard. The next year, I was a seventh grader on the eighth grade team. Again, I was the star of the team. Again, I prayed every night for the MVP. Again, I was denied. This time, the school had a shortage of money and had to eliminate the awards ceremony altogether. The cavalier words, "Sorry kiddo, maybe next year," were all I received for my talents and my prayers. I was devastated. After that, I stopped praying entirely, and the forsaken feeling I harbored would continue to fester into adulthood.

What might seem like a trivial event, in retrospect, can nonetheless have an enormous impact on a child. In this case, it caused my belief system to take shape. How about you? Do you know what shaped your belief system? Do you know why you believe what you believe? Are your beliefs based on evaluation and soul-searching, or on the fact that you were, "brought up that way?" Try to figure it out. You might even have a little league experience of your own. By the way, I'm still pissed about not getting that MVP trophy! I just don't blame God for it anymore. After all, as Pat Boone says, "God isn't a short-order cook."

I am too smart for fairy tales

After seventh grade, I pretty much ignored God, or the subject of God for that matter. And as I got older, I developed a hefty cynicism towards the topic as well. When someone broached the idea of God in my presence, I would just snicker and write them off as naive or silly. I figured the notion of God was the necessity of the ignorant, who needed to believe in this fantasy to get through life. I, on the other hand, was too brilliant to allow myself to be fooled. I was not going to be duped by this Supreme Being myth, as was the case with the other ninety-five percent of the people on the planet. Damn, I was arrogant! But I was outwardly content with being arrogant and closed off to other possibilities. After all, what if I were to acknowledge that in fact there was a God, or Supreme Being, or Higher Power. Then I would actually be accountable for all my bad behavior. Heck, that's not convenient!

Like other like-minded geniuses, I would often poke fun at the notion of a godly figure, sitting on a throne up in the clouds somewhere. How absurd! But any concept can be satirized this way, in order to make it appear ridiculous. Comedians wouldn't exist if this were not the case. And when you really think about it, does the "big bang" theory sound any less absurd? A bunch of elements were floating through space and then, "oops" they collided, and voila--earth is formed. Then of course, some single celled organisms magically popped up, eventually "evolving" into blah, blah, blah, and "poof," here we are. Of course!

I had a dream a few years ago that deeply influenced my views on the mystery of creation. It was more vivid than any other dream I've ever had. In fact, it had such an impact on solidifying my faith in God, that I am tempted to call it a vision, or a glimpse, instead of a dream.

The dream began when I walked into my house, and saw Rod Stewart sitting at my kitchen table. Thank goodness he was just sitting, and not serenading me with, "If you want my body, and you think I'm sexy..." Anyway, in the dream he represented a wise, celestial figure, not a rock star. On the table, beside him, sat a sumptuous apple pie. Its aroma made me salivate. I proceeded to eat a piece, taking care to taste the various different flavors of apple, cinnamon, and sugar. I then asked Rod, "Did somebody make this pie?" He replied, "Well, certainly! Given a billion years and a billion apples, do you think such a masterpiece could have been created by accident?"

As soon as I awoke, I felt like I had been given an extraordinary gift. Then within seconds, I felt enlightened. I suddenly realized why witnessing my son's birth was a "religious experience" for me. I could now intellectualize what I felt in my heart, inside that hospital room on May 3rd, 1998. If I reject the existence of God, then I would consequently have to accept the unacceptable—that my beautiful son, along with a myriad of other wondrous things in the universe, is the result of some cosmic accident. In my heart, my mind and my soul, I know this is not the case.

Intelligent but still ignorant

Did you ever meet a very intelligent person who could regurgitate all sorts of facts and figures on cue, but had the emotional capacity of a tomato can? I have met plenty, none of whom I would go to for spiritual advice. If I have a concern that is black-and-white, this is the sort of person that I consult. But to gain any insights about a concept like faith, it's usually more fruitful to go elsewhere.

I recently met a woman named Lea, who claimed she was an Atheist. When I asked her why, she said because an old boyfriend—supposedly a modern day Einstein—was an Atheist. Apparently, she valued his opinions so much, that his views became her views. I suppose she figured, "This guy is smarter than me. He must be right." Blindly taking on the views of a spouse, parent, or close friend, is a very common phenomenon. And for good reason—it gives the person one less thing to think about.

The thing I found curious was that Lea said she was uncomfortable talking about God. It was a "sore subject." Even more peculiar to me was her admitted guilt at not getting her kids baptized. If she truly did not believe in God, then why did she feel guilty? The conflict inside of her was obvious. Her opinion that God does not exist did not jibe with what she truly felt inside. I told her that I thought she should examine this conflict.

I offered this advice because she needed help. Even before our discussion about God, she lamented that she needed inspiration in her life. Although she appeared to be a dynamic and vivacious person, she felt empty inside. Going through a divorce and raising two children alone had left her feeling helpless and lost. I knew that only faith could help her find her way. So I offered my advice on how to develop a little faith, and with nothing to lose, she followed it.

After facing her inner conflict, and watching a few sunrises, Lea agreed to hang out with various friends of mine, on a few separate occasions. These friends are true-believers, but at the same time, they are not obnoxious about cramming the subject of God down everyone's throat. If asked, they will tell you how they feel and what they believe, but they will not be presumptuous enough to tell you what you should feel and believe. I think that is why Lea felt so comfortable talking to them. When all was said and done, Lea admitted that she had a sense of inner peace and optimism that no amount of logic could explain. That alone was more than enough for me to know that our efforts were successful.

How strong her faith in God is now, if in fact she has developed any faith at all, is her own personal business. What's important to me is that Lea, who no longer refers to herself as an Atheist, has filled the void inside of her with contentment. I will leave it up to you to contemplate the true source of that contentment.

Resistant thinkers

Back in the day, not only was I a know-it-all, but when it came to God, I was a "resistant thinker." Not only did I resist accepting other viewpoints, I resisted hearing them in the first place. Some people are resistant thinkers in general. These folks are perfectly comfortable confined to their own, narrow view of the world. Think about it. We're all familiar with the person who hates the food that he never tasted, or abhors the movie that he never actually saw. Unless these folks are omniscient, they're probably depriving themselves of many terrific things. This goes back to the premise, that if you're going to believe in something—especially something of universal significance—make sure you know why you believe in it. And to know why, you must seek out the answers; answers that often lie outside of your comfort zone.

For me personally, during my quest for the truth, what troubled me the most was not understanding all the answers.

In the past, I would discard things that I could not comprehend or make sense of. But just because we do not understand something, does not make it any less true. When I read Wayne Dyer's, *Wisdom of the Ages*, I came across a quote by William Jennings Bryan that encapsulates this idea exquisitely:

> *I have observed the power of the watermelon seed. It has the power of drawing from the ground and through itself 200,000 times its weight. When you can tell me how it takes this material and out of it colors an outside surface beyond imitation of art, and then forms inside of it a white rind and within that again a red heart, thickly inlaid with black seeds, each one of which in turn is capable of drawing through itself 200,000 times its weight—when you can explain to me the mystery of the watermelon, you can ask me to explain the mystery of God.*

It is human nature to question what we do not understand. We also have a tendency to doubt what we cannot see. I will defer to Deepak Chopra's, *The Deeper Wound* to illustrate the folly in this way of thinking:

> *Things aren't real because you can see and touch them. That is an illusion of the senses. A granite cliff is real because invisible forces hold together invisible packets of energy. No one has ever seen gravity or the curvature of space, yet their existence is far more secure than granite, which will dissolve and cease to exist billions of years before gravity does. All the most real things, in fact, are invisible. No one has ever touched time. Truth leaves no fingerprints. Love escapes the five senses.*

Finding a purpose in it all

Many people believe in God, but that alone does not necessarily empower them to overcome great hardships. I think one reason for this is they fail to see a purpose to their suffering. What an injustice it would be if our suffering was just a random event. Well, that's how I used to feel anyway. I mean, how unfair is it that I endure great tribulations, while my buddy, John Q. Public, is happy and healthy? Shouldn't I get bonus points at the Pearly Gates?

In the *Art of Happiness*, by the Dalai Lama and Howard Cutler, the authors cite an example of how vital it is to find a purpose in one's suffering. Victor Frankl was a Jewish psychiatrist imprisoned by the Nazis in World War II. He used his horrific experience to gain insight into how people survived these atrocities. He asserted that survival was not based on youth or physical strength, but on the strength of one's purpose. Mr. Frankl was quoted as saying, "Man is ready and willing to shoulder any suffering as long as he can see a meaning in it." I think he was absolutely right. Just think about it. If a maniac abducted you and removed one of your kidneys, just to amuse himself, the pain and suffering you would endure would last forever. On the other hand, if your sibling needed a kidney to survive, you would offer it to him or her with glee. The vital purpose of the second scenario makes a possibly traumatic event, not only bearable, but joyful.

When a person is in the throes of tragedy or hardship, it is often impossible to see a light at the end of the tunnel. Think about how many friends you have consoled after a divorce or breakup. Almost always, they will say, "I can't imagine ever loving another person again," or "I can't conceive of this pain ever going away." Perhaps you personally have felt like this once or twice. In the midst of grief, it is hard to imagine a way out. Finding a purpose in it is an even greater challenge. But invariably, after the cloud of despair disperses, the person realizes that there is light at the end of the tunnel. And perhaps many years down the road, they see the purpose after all. Maybe the person was afforded the opportunity to move on to a more meaningful relationship, or deeper love. Or maybe that individual moved out from behind the shadow of their spouse, to become a strong, independent, and fulfilled person.

Irrespective of the circumstances, our hardships allow us to learn, and ultimately grow. A quote from Allyson Jones in *Chicken Soup for the Unsinkable Soul*, says it best: "If I could wish for my life to be perfect, it would be tempting, but I would have to decline, for life would no longer teach me anything." The lesson in our suffering may not always be easy to find, but I assure you, it's there.

That's exactly what I told my cousin Vincent when he was going through an ugly divorce several months ago. He was so miserable and full of self-pity that I knew convincing him to find a purpose for his pain would be a daunting task. So I started discussing the general subject of divorce to get him to look past his own situation for a while. I got him to accept the fact that divorce, or any other type of loss, is a pervasive part of the human condition. No one on this earth can escape loss. The loss of love as a result of death or separation is more than just a small part of life. It's ubiquitous and it's inevitable. Not only that, but each and every one of us is guaranteed to deal with it at every turn.

After he fully acknowledged these facts, I started the questioning phase. I asked, "Since loss is such an integral part of life, don't you think God has a purpose for it?" He reluctantly agreed, but he complained, "I will never understand or know His purpose, so why should I waste my time looking for it?" Well, sometimes it is more important to know what is NOT the answer, than to know what IS the answer. Accordingly, I posed this question: "Do you think God's purpose is to see you suffer indefinitely, and quit living a fulfilling life?" His silence spoke volumes. He then realized that if he allowed this divorce to ruin his life, he was not only failing himself and those around him, but he was failing God as well.

Although he certainly was not "cured" by our conversation, he took the most important step on the road to defying despair—the first one. Before, he believed that there was nothing he could do to feel better, so he didn't even bother trying. With a little faith, however, there was a reason to make the effort. Now, he was ready to find some inspiration. (See Chapter Eight.)

Deeper meaning

Finding an "earthly" purpose for our travails can get us through the unthinkable. But in my case, finding a deeper purpose to my suffering was more significant to me. In the *Spirits Book*, by Allan Kardec, he writes that each life on earth is a "trial." If one endures great hardships in life, "without murmuring," he will learn enough to advance in the afterlife. According to Kardec, the greater the hardship, the greater the opportunity for spiritual growth. Conversely, if one is afforded every luxury without challenges, or does not help others with his good fortune, he cannot advance.

Kardec believed that we continue to repeat these trials (different earthly lives) until we reach a certain level of divinity. If you believe as he did, you have found the deeper purpose in your suffering. If not, don't fret. There are still many insights to be drawn from his body of work. Whether you believe in reincarnation, or heaven, or whatever else, Mr. Kardec's teachings contain universal truths and provoke meaningful thought.

Incidentally, in *Reincarnation and Biology*, by Dr. Ian Stevenson, there is compelling information supporting the theory of reincarnation. If you decide to read it, don't worry, there's nothing in there about coming back to life as an earthworm. Honestly though, when you consider that many of the world's greatest philosophers, including Plato, believed in some form of reincarnation, the subject is at least worth a look.

Many scholars even believe that reincarnation is totally consistent with the Bible and the teachings of Jesus Christ. The *Gospel According to Spiritism,* by Allan Kardec, offers a very persuasive view on the subject, which is beyond the scope of this book. In western culture, there is a stigma attached to the idea of reincarnation, for various historical reasons. I believe the most significant reason relates to a society's need for law and order. Historically, religion has been used as a tool to dissuade people from engaging in undesirable behaviors that cause harm to the society. However, the prospect of eternal damnation in the pits of hell proved to be a much greater deterrent to bad behavior, than the idea of getting a second chance through reincarnation. So for practical purposes alone, the notion of reincarnation fell by the wayside. Read up a little on what I've discussed—you may be surprised at what you learn.

There are many divergent philosophies, but the differences in ideology do not concern me in the context of finding meaning in it all. What is imperative for me is realizing that my suffering will be relatively brief, and that no matter what, there will be something more after this life. And when that time comes, I will reap the benefits gained from my painful experiences. The idea of suffering leading to spiritual growth seems to be a universal theme, regardless of the philosophy or religion one subscribes to. But of course, every now and then, doubt creeps in. On these occasions, reading this passage from the *Deeper Wound*, by Deepak Chopra, is one of the ways that I reaffirm my belief that there is something more:

> *Try to imagine your own death and then try to imagine your own birth. No matter how hard you try, both are impossible in any corner of your consciousness. There is no hint of a beginning or an ending. Inside we all feel ourselves as always having lived, which is true.*

Belief without the trust

Most people on the planet believe in some sort of Higher Power, who is all-knowing and all-powerful. However, this belief is rarely accompanied by trust. Those few that do truly trust in God are the ones that have the power to triumph over any adversity. God gave us life, along with everything that comes with it, for a reason. If God had no purpose for our suffering, life would amount to nothing more than a cruel sort of crap game for His amusement. I for one believe that human existence has a much more profound significance than that. Trust God—I think He knows what He's doing.

Unfortunately, even for the true believer, that trust can erode rather quickly when life seems inordinately cruel. I recently met an incredible woman who has dealt with more tragedy in her life than most of us could even fathom. When Gaby was fourteen years old, she was raped by a clergyman, who was a close friend of the family. A few years later, she married a womanizer who physically abused her on a regular basis. She faced more tragedy many years later, when her eighteen year old son was shot and killed. Two years later, her youngest daughter died of cancer. I'm not even going to mention her own health problems. While most people would have been institutionalized by this point, Gaby continued to be an optimistic and spirited person. She remains that way today.

If you ask her how she can be so strong, she'll tell you that her life is in God's hands. Her energies are only directed towards the things in life that she has control over. She says, "God will sort out the rest." Gaby's belief and trust in God is unshakeable, which is why she continues to thrive in the face of life's worst tragedies. This simple, unassuming woman possesses a power that makes her invincible. If you trust in God even half as much as Gaby, you will possess all the power you need to defy despair.

The power of prayer

When I concluded that my suffering had a purpose, I threw in the towel. Now I'm just biding my time until the next life. All right, you got me; I did no such thing! After all, I want to live the happiest and most productive life I can—right now. Besides, I don't think the purpose of suffering is to give in to it. There are never any rewards for quitters, in this life, or the next. We have an obligation to use every ounce of effort, and every resource available to overcome our suffering. The end result of this effort may take on many different forms. In my case, I want to be cured. And if that's not possible, then I want to feel as good as I can. And on the days when my body feels like frappéd crap, I still want to be emotionally strong and optimistic.

Praying has been instrumental to me in this respect. Now this is not one person's delusions, mind you. I assure you, there is more to prayer than just wishful thinking. In addition to the obvious spiritual and mental benefits that praying can provide, its curative benefits are well documented. Since there is such an abundance of studies and information on this subject, it is impossible to deny that the power of prayer is real. Do a search on the Internet and you'll have reading material for a month. You'll find everything from prayer speeding the recovery of cardiac patients, to prayer doubling the replication rate of single celled organisms in petri dishes. Even scientists cannot dispute the facts. Instead, they can only debate as to how "on earth" this phenomenon is possible. None of us can say we know the answer for certain. What I can say, however, is that I've never once heard the words, "Oh man, all this praying is really making me feel like crap." By the way, just as a side note, if you're praying for an MVP trophy, all bets are off!

Healings

Stay with me now, because I'm going to take this one step further. A few years ago, I met a woman, and we began a friendship. Upon hearing of my illness, she told me of a miracle she had witnessed. Her uncle had been debilitated by Multiple Sclerosis, and was unable to walk. She told me that as a last resort, he went to a priest with the ability to heal. According to her, at the healing mass, her uncle was spontaneously healed, and was dancing on tables at a party several weeks later. Now if you're anything like the old me, you are looking for every possible explanation for this, other than it being a genuine miracle. Or maybe you think it's simply bogus. I won't hold it against you. Hey, I doubted it myself—that's why I checked it out first-hand.

Over the course of several months, I participated in a few of these healing masses. Was I healed? Unfortunately not. But I must admit, I was heartened by the atmosphere of strength, faith, compassion, and determination. Do I think anyone else was healed? Honestly, yes. And I'll tell you why. During one particular mass, there was a teen-aged deaf girl, along with her parents, sitting two rows behind me. Towards the end of the mass, the priest asked if there was a deaf girl in the crowd. She stood up at her parents urging, and the priest beckoned for her to go to him. He proceeded to touch her ears for several seconds, and then asked, "Can you hear?" She meekly responded, "Yes." I looked at her face as she returned back passed my row. She had a look of pure befuddlement. Her parents greeted her with a frantic barrage of, "Is it true, is it true?" The girl broke down in tears, nodding her head in the affirmative. The three of them wept.

Now I consider myself very adept at sniffing out B.S., so if this was all some staged performance, not only will I eat my hat, but I'll eat my coat, my shoes, and my socks too. I have no doubt that what I saw was genuine. My two friends that accompanied me to the mass concur, as well. Regardless of what truly happened that day, I am grateful for having been given another reason to hope.

A few weeks after the mass, one of the friends that I just mentioned revealed something amazing to me. Evidently, what transpired at the mass was more significant than I could have imagined. Her experience occurred towards the end of the service, when the priest had asked a handful of people, including the deaf girl, to stand up and be healed. But when he asked if the lady with pain in her ovaries would stand, no one came forward. I remember the priest persisting, but still no one moved. Now, several weeks later, my friend was admitting to me that since that moment, she no longer felt the pain caused by endometriosis— a condition of the ovaries.

She told me that she felt guilty for receiving any benefit from the mass, because her only wish was for me to be healed. My selfless friend did not want any healing energy to be "wasted" on her. That's why she did not stand up. Another twist to this saga is that the entire mass did not reflect her religious views whatsoever. Even though she is Muslim, she put her personal beliefs aside in order to give me emotional support. I am so glad that she was rewarded for being such a beautiful and giving person. Maybe the lesson here is that the manner in which we pray is far less important than the love we offer through our prayers.

Faith in Yourself

Those of you who tend to be scientifically minded can relax, because I'm finished discussing the spiritual realm. Let's assume for a second that God is not part of the equation. We're all on our own in the world, with nothing to depend on but the faith in ourselves. Can one overcome despair without necessarily believing that they're being helped by some heavenly force? Of course.

Power of the mind

The power of the mind is manifest in almost everything we see or touch; rocketships, artificial hearts, the Internet, etcetera. For most of us, it's even hard to comprehend that such things are possible. Yet we tend to overlook the fact that these technologies were not just dropped on our laps by the stork. They are all products of the human mind. There seems to be no limit to what the mind can do. Certainly, this power includes the ability to overcome grief. And moreover, why should the ability to improve ailments of the body be out of the realm of possibility? Is it that much of a leap?

There can be no doubt that certain supernatural phenomena exist. Some people prefer to believe that many of these phenomena—healings, ESP, and the like—can be attributed to the inordinate power of the mind. Not much argument here. But are these awesome abilities exclusive to only a select few, or can it be developed by the ordinary Joe? One phenomenon that leads me to believe the latter is the "placebo effect."

Placebo effect

What is it? Here's an example. A woman is about to get major stomach surgery, which obviously requires the use of anesthesia to numb the pain. But instead of getting the real anesthetic, she receives an injection of saline solution. The salt content of the solution makes the injection burn, fooling the woman into thinking the drug is very powerful. She proceeds to undergo the operation without a peep. So despite having received no anesthetic, she endured stomach surgery without feeling any pain. In essence, her mind allowed her to accomplish an unimaginable feat. Granted, she had to be fooled in order to accomplish it. But the fact remains, her mind possessed the ability to profoundly influence her body. If the mind possesses this inherent power, maybe with extraordinary commitment we can unlock it somehow.

I am so intrigued by this phenomenon that I never get tired of reading about it. Doctors and scientists seem to be equally intrigued, because they can't sufficiently explain it. One more example that blows my mind involves the drug minoxidil, used to treat baldness. This drug is the only topical FDA approved drug for regrowing hair. On each package of Rogaine—the drug's brand name—the manufacturer provides results of clinical studies that supposedly prove minoxidil's effectiveness. The study shows that 26 percent of the minoxidil group had *dense* hair regrowth, compared to 11 percent in the placebo group. Do you know what that really means? It means that 11 out of every 100 men grew considerable amounts of hair on their bald heads—just with the power of their minds! Furthermore, 31 out of 100 men in the placebo group had at least light regrowth! If some spiritual guru claimed that 11 percent of his bald students substantially regrow hair on their heads through meditation, he would be ridiculed. But when the same results occur in the context of a clinical study, we tend to accept it, without trying to understand what it really means.

I have personally experienced how powerful, and in this instance entertaining, the placebo effect can be. When I was eighteen years old, a friend and I offered to make dinner for our girlfriends. Being lovestruck teenagers, we desperately wanted to impress them. So we told them we were preparing Mexican food, and that we would get a bottle of wine also. After slaving over a hot stove, we went out to get the wine. Well, as unusual as it was in those days, the joker at the liquor store asked for identification. Of all the days to be "proofed!" So we had to move to an alternate plan. We quickly decided that sparkling grape juice might be a cool alternative to wine. You know, to make us look cultured. Well, the girls eventually arrived, we had dinner, and everything was going well. My friend and I noticed, however, that the girls were acting strange. Their eyes were glazed over, they were extremely giddy, and they even walked a little wobbly. Oh man, were we leveled when we realized that they were acting drunk! The bottle of grape juice was sitting right on the table, but they never looked closely at it. And my friend and I never mentioned the grape juice, because we didn't want to look like dweebs for not being able to get the wine. It was a blast watching the girls "get drunk" on grape juice. To this day, I laugh every time I think about it.

Love can move mountains

They say that love can move mountains. If you are not a big fan of metaphors, then let's just say that love can give people enormous power. Since we all have the capacity to love, I believe we all have the potential power to "move mountains." The following example conveys just how extraordinary that power can be.

My friend Tia was twenty-two years old when her younger sister became gravely ill. This poor girl suffered immensely over the next two years until she fell into a coma. Living in another state at the time, Tia rushed to be at her sister's side. After a few days, the family and the medical staff decided to remove the life support system. But Tia refused to let go, pleading with her sister not to leave her.

Tears ran down the comatose girl's face as if she was aware of Tia's presence. After the ventilator was removed, Tia stubbornly urged her sister to hang on—and she did. A week later, the doctor's decided to euthanize the girl with a drug that stops the heart. Her heart refused to cooperate. Finally after another week passed, the family's priest convinced Tia to return home and let her sister find peace. By the time Tia arrived back home, her sister had passed away.

Although most of us have not experienced a miracle such as this, we can certainly relate to the profound love shared by these two sisters. If so, then we can imagine how powerful love can make us. What I want you to realize is that love does not just hand-deliver a gift-wrapped package of power. Instead, it allows us to unleash the power that all of us already possess within ourselves. Any one of us can move mountains, and true love continues to show us how.

Meditation

As I stated earlier, prayer has been an integral part of my formula against despair. But this practice does not necessarily have to involve praying to God. Many people derive great benefit from simply meditating. Just lying still, relaxing your breathing, and taking a brief respite from your troubles can be extremely soothing. I personally like to use imagery when I meditate. Frequently, I imagine pure white light penetrating my head and engulfing all the darkness that represents my Parkinson's Disease. While riding my exercise bike, I also engage in a form of meditation. In this instance, I imagine the blood in my veins being pumped through my heart and into my brain, carrying nutrients and healing energy. Obviously, I'm looking for an energizing effect in this case, instead of a relaxing one.

On occasion, meditation can have a big payoff. A few years back, I saw an amazing story on the news. This little boy, about seven years old, had been diagnosed with a form of terminal blood cancer. Apparently, it was aggressive, making the prognosis grim. Possessing an unbridled imagination, and devoid of the cynicism of most adults, the boy immersed himself into a fantasy. Every day, he fantasized that there was a fighter jet cruising around in his bloodstream, blowing all his cancer cells to smithereens. He was so entrenched in his fantasy that it eventually became a reality. When he returned to the doctor's office, his cancer was completely gone. Did the cancer eventually come back? Who knows. Either way though, the boy accomplished something extraordinary, and in doing so, blessed everyone with an invaluable gift—hope.

First-hand knowledge

We all have the ability to tap into our mind's great potential. I know this because I, an ordinary Joe, once accomplished something amazing with my mind. Many years ago, I was a student at a highly specialized and intensive martial arts school for adults. It was private, and by recommendation only. Mental focus and concentration were vital to each student's development. After five years of intense training, the top students, which included me, needed to pass a test in order to advance to the next level. A one-inch thick board was mounted upright in front of each student. We were to place our fingers lightly against the board, with the thumb up and the pinky down. The task was to break the board without removing our fingers from it, or cocking our arms back. In essence, we had to break the board by merely snapping our wrists. To perform the "one inch power punch," as coined by Bruce Lee, a person needed extraordinary mental focus.

On the night of the test, all the students were very well-prepared. However, the first four students failed, two of which were well-built, two-hundred pound men. Obviously, physical strength was useless for this test. Success was contingent solely on the mind's ability to generate sufficient force in the fingertips, and allow it to explode outward. The fifth student, a ninety-five pound woman with wrists as thick as a carrot, proved that notion by breaking the board. I knew then that it wasn't impossible. But when my turn came, I failed. My attempt was so poor, it felt like I was trying to chop down an oak tree with my tongue. Then it was my brother's turn, and to my amazement, he broke the board. I was proud of him, but at the same time I felt a surge of anger; anger that I was not capable of doing what my brother had just accomplished.

The sibling rivalry phenomenon was in full effect, so I focused all my energy toward the task at hand. Since each of us were given two chances, I had one last opportunity. I was brimming with such intense resolution that no thought, other than breaking that board, entered my mind. I didn't even notice that everyone else failed on their second attempts. When my second chance came, nothing else existed in the world besides me and this wooden obstacle. With my entire body vibrating with determination, I once again placed my fingers on the board, concentrated, and my fist exploded forward. I swear to you, the board not only broke, but it shattered. Several pieces of wood shot out like bullets. The same wood that minutes before felt like an oak tree was now obliterated. I just stood there in awe.

I'll never forget what I accomplished with my mind that night, so many years ago. But that was only a practice run for what I am facing today. I haven't quite obliterated Parkinson's Disease yet, but I'm working on it. It's just a matter of time before I find the right focus.

Acknowledging the extraordinary

If you're anything like I used to be, by now you are probably knee-deep in "yeah buts." "Yeah but, people exaggerate." "Yeah but, everyone is just lying for publicity, or to gain something." "Yeah but, the boy's cancer could have come back." If this is the case, I must warn you; you are in danger of becoming a yeah-butthead. Look in the mirror. If you see evidence of this happening, sit down and force yourself to acknowledge one unavoidable fact—extraordinary things do happen.

I am certain that extraordinary events, such as healings, do occur. The question is, "Can something extraordinary happen to me?" My particular shortcoming in this area has been the tendency to sell myself short. At times, I think about the many remarkable individuals that have not been able to physically overcome Parkinson's Disease. How can I presume to think that I am more special than Muhammad Ali, for example? Am I more worthy than my personal hero, Michael J. Fox? If they can't do it, how in the world can I? But after refocusing, I always come back to the truth: I must not presume anything. The truth is that although MJF is a gifted man, maybe I possess one quality or ability that he doesn't. How can I presume to know what his belief system is for that matter?

Besides, what about the remarkable individuals that

have accomplished the "impossible?" There are plenty of public figures whose stories of overcoming physical maladies are nothing short of miraculous. The first one involves Magic Johnson. In 1991, the basketball star announced he had contracted the HIV virus. From that day forward, his brilliant smile never dimmed; his commitment to helping others never waned; and his zest for life never faltered. He was such a model of strength, I wondered if he knew something that the rest of us didn't know. Today, it's more than twelve years later, and he is still symptom-free. From the start, the disease had no chance against him mentally. Apparently, HIV is no match for Magic physically, either.

Then, there is Lance Armstrong, one of the world's top cyclists. His story is one that makes you shake your head every time you think about it. In 1996, he was stricken with deadly testicular cancer, which quickly spread to his lungs and brain. He was given a twenty percent chance of survival. Five short months after his diagnosis, he was training again. Now, an astonishing five consecutive Tour de France titles later, he dominates his sport. Over the years, I have learned of many examples of people's strength to survive. But to me, what makes this case so incredible is that Lance Armstrong had the immeasurable strength, not only to survive, but to transcend.

It's up to you to decide if these success stories are nothing but freak occurrences, or something more. Whatever the case may be, I for one will continue to believe that I can use my mind to benefit my body. It can't hurt.

Power of negative thinking

What can hurt, however, is negative thinking. Yes,

sometimes it's difficult to be positive when life kicks you in the groin, but bitching and moaning sure as heck doesn't make things better. One thing that really troubles me is the woe-is-me folks. You know the ones I'm referring to? They're the ones who whine when they talk, as if they were in the process of dying. Usually these people fret and complain about things like the terrible head cold that their pet hamster, Fluffy is dealing with. Or they say, "terrible" every single time you ask them how they're doing. And most likely, they complain about a host of other things that they shouldn't waste energy worrying about. Fluffy's head cold notwithstanding, many people do indeed have reasons to complain. The question is, what good does it do?

For the person dealing with an illness, the next question should be, what harm can it do? The harm that negative thoughts and words can have on one's emotional health should be painfully obvious. Especially after losing all your friends, because your incessant whining penetrates their skulls like a knife. Even when not expressed outwardly, negative thoughts can affect our mood and behavior in ways we might never expect. Did you ever have a dream, in which your spouse cheated on you or humiliated you in some way? You might not have even noticed, but the day after, you probably were cold, or even nasty with him/her. And the cause of this behavior was nothing more than a silly, fabricated, negative thought—in the form of a dream no less. Reality can remain the same, and yet one erroneous thought can impact a person's feelings and actions. We may not be able to control what we dream about, but we can definitely try to limit the negativity that we consciously dwell on.

In addition to emotional repercussions, a person who is

ill needs to be concerned with the physical harm negativity can cause. A plethora of empirical evidence unequivocally proves that this concern is justified. I think we all accept it as a given that negative thoughts and attitudes can affect the body. But I don't think most people appreciate the degree to which this occurs. In Wayne Dyer's *Wisdom of the Ages*, he asserts that mental attitude can literally impact the atoms and molecules that comprise the body. He goes on to quote Deepak Chopra, M.D. as saying, "Happy thoughts make happy molecules." Chopra points out that the chemical composition of tears of joy varies dramatically from the chemical composition of tears of sadness. Cool, huh?

But don't just take Dr. Chopra's word for it. Let's briefly look at the process by which negative emotions lead to physical harm to our bodies. It all starts with a tiny gland called the hypothalamus, located within the brain. This powerful gland releases a variety of hormones in response to different emotions. And of course, our emotions are based on our thoughts.

When we are in love, for instance, our minds are filled with fond and amorous thoughts about our significant other. These thoughts foster feelings of love within us. Thus, when we are with that person, or even think about him/her, our bodies release endorphins which make us feel all warm and fuzzy. The flip side of this lovefest would be the body's response to fear. The primary reaction of the hypothalamus, in this case, is the release of cortisol, which has the potential to heal wounds by alleviating inflammation. The evolutionary purpose to this response was to protect ourselves against injury, in anticipation of a fight for food or territory. But in the 21st century, our sources of fear have expanded to include far less dangerous circumstances. However, the hypothalamus pumps out cortisol just the same, no matter what the source may be. So even if your fear is strawberry shortcake, the hypothalamus will do its job nonetheless. Unfortunately, excess cortisol has harmful effects on the body. When a person is worried, anxious, or afraid, the release of cortisol suspends digestion, which acidifies the blood, raises blood pressure and heart rate, and tenses up the muscles. Incidentally, cortisol is also an exerciser's worst enemy because it breaks down muscle tissue. Apparently, cortisol was doing a number on my body for many years. Now that it's not, my body feels, performs, and looks infinitely better.

It goes without saying that cortisol was not meant to be roaming around the body very frequently, or for very long periods of time. With respect to those people who are constantly thinking the sky is falling, the implications to their health are foreboding. The next time you are brooding over something trivial, remember that you'll be joined by your buddy cortisol—whose effects are anything but trivial.

I hope we all agree that negative thoughts can harm us physically and emotionally. So what can we do to control them? Being aware of the futility and insanity of constantly rehashing our problems is a good start. In *Awaken the Giant Within*, Tony Robbins sums up the lunacy of negative thinking with an analogy: "Have you ever gone to an awful movie? Would you go back to that awful movie hundreds of times? Of course not. Why? Because it wouldn't feel good to do this! Then why would you go back to the awful movies in your head on a regular basis? Why watch yourself in your least favorite roles, playing against your least favorite leading lady or man?

Why play out disasters or bad decisions again and again?"

Indeed, there is no plausible reason. But believe me, I know that keeping negativity at bay is easier said than done. All I can say is try to be vigilant. When you realize you're being a sad sack, ask yourself if ruminating over negative thoughts is benefiting you or harming you. Over time, it has become second nature for me to question these uninvited intruders. Consequently, most adverse thoughts that enter my mind are automatically supplanted by uplifting ones. "I can't" automatically becomes "I will." "I feel like crap" necessarily becomes "I will feel better." "I wish I was able to..." gets converted into "How can I improve..." And the list goes on.

Empowerment at worst

Okay, so we've established that I have faith in myself and the power of my mind. Furthermore, I meditate, explore all possibilities, and think happy-happy, joy-joy thoughts. I bet you are wondering what I hope to accomplish. Well obviously, my ultimate goal is to feel better physically. In the form of being completely healed would be nice, but truthfully, I'll take whatever improvement to my health I can get. And what am I left with if I come up short for now? Empowerment. What I have definitely realized is that trying new approaches to beating my illness has given me a sense of control. Even if nothing "works" in the way that I would like, I still feel like I am dictating the process. The flip side would be to just sit back and feel helpless. And helplessness leads to hopelessness. If someone were to ask me how to beat despair in one word, I would have to say, "hope." I will continue to try anything and everything in the hopes that eventually I will rid myself of this disease.

No such thing as false hope

Some will argue—most likely in a whiny voice—that talk of healing yourself, and improving your health with the mind, is just giving people false hope. They might further contend that one shouldn't pin his hopes on extraordinary things that occur so rarely. <Sigh> Well if these folks never do anything unless there is a written guarantee of success, then they may have a leg to stand on. My guess, however, is that most of them pin their hopes on much sillier things than improving their health. For example, how many millions of people in this country play Lotto on a regular basis? Why do they spend their hard-earned money to play? Because it's likely that they will win? Obviously not. Despite the astronomical odds against them, and total lack of control in the process, they continue to hope against hope, week after week after week. They continue playing because there exists the possibility—however minute—that they could win. And lo and behold, lucky winners emerge every week. What do you think *they* would say about false hope?

Keep in mind, also, that the payoff in the Lotto example is just money. The payoff in trying new ways to strengthen your body is exponentially greater. Some of you out there will just have to trust me on this one. Maybe it's just me, but if one can go to the ends of the earth to make money, or win money, shouldn't a greater effort be made in regards to health? I hope I haven't said anything to give people false hope, but frankly, in this context, I would take false hope over no hope any day.

Chapter Eight

Inspiration

Needless to say, travails such as having a serious illness, can make it difficult to even get through the day. During my period of study and self-evaluation, I tried to figure out what motivates people to persevere, in spite of great pain, debilitating fatigue, or mental anguish. Believe me, during the times when I feel too tired to scratch an itch, or when my neck hurts as if it were in a vice grip, even the simplest tasks seem daunting. So when I am weak, physically or emotionally, I need to find the inspiration to carry on.

Finding Your Sources

In my powerlifting example that I mentioned earlier, the main source of the individual's inspiration was the need for self-esteem, derived from a sense of power and achievement. But what if he fails to reach his goal? Or better yet, what if he gives up and becomes a ballerina for the traveling circus? No biggie, right? Life will continue. But when we're talking about a case where life may not continue, or continue in a much less qualitative way, how does one muster up the will to go on? What inspires a person to persevere through pain and sickness, when every fiber of his being is begging him to quit? Stick around, because I may have a few ideas for you.

Loved ones

In order to cope with any tragedy, one needs a strong support system. Usually, this consists of family and friends. Just knowing that you can count on someone when times get tough is a great comfort. They can also be a source of inspiration when grief starts to suffocate you and zap your will to fight.

I am extremely fortunate to have a very supportive family that sustains me. When I was broke, my brother helped me out financially, which gave me the opportunity to focus all of my energies on my health. He sacrificed many luxuries just so I wouldn't be burdened with the stress of not being able to pay my bills. This type of financial support, however, cannot last indefinitely. People have their own bills to pay. But I have been lucky enough to get tremendous emotional support as well. My cousin, Vincent is a big reason for that. Whatever I need, whenever I need it, he always comes through without complaining or judging. The many things he does to make my life easier shows a caring that inspires me to clear any hurdle.

I will not let my brother or my cousin down by allowing Parkinson's Disease to beat me. Instead, I will do everything I can to ensure that their efforts are not in vain. Right now, I have good reason to celebrate; I have defied despair. But I vow to continue the fight until the day that I have rid myself of Parkinson's Disease. Then, all of us will celebrate.

My parents have also been troopers. It is torturous to

see your child suffer. That applies no matter how old the "child" happens to be. My parents are very supportive and giving, but they are hurting inside. And you know what? I'm not going to do anything to exacerbate their pain. That of course includes, sulking, complaining, bitching, and moaning. But additionally, that means I will do everything in my power to be strong, and stay healthy. Some people dream of one day being able to buy their parents a nice house, or send them on a one month cruise. I used to wish for that too. Now, the best that I can do is offer them the comfort of knowing that their son is flourishing, despite his obstacles. I have a funny feeling they would welcome that over a cruise, any day. I assume that goes for the house too, but don't quote me on it.

If you think your family is not being as supportive as you would like, maybe you need to communicate better. The first couple of years after my diagnosis, I bottled everything up inside. Consequently, I felt isolated and misunderstood. How were my loved ones supposed to be supportive if they were totally in the dark? No one can know exactly how you feel but you, so don't assume your family will intuitively understand what you're going through. You don't have to complain; simply communicate. Trust me, they will appreciate it.

I am also fortunate enough to have a few great friends. I do, however, deserve some kudos for choosing them as friends in the first place. If you're lucky enough to be married, then you have the ultimate friend. Since I'm single, I can only imagine how intensely inspirational and supportive a loving spouse can be. But I'll tell you, my friends haven't been too shabby in that department either. Friends are those patient people who listen to you sob on the phone, when they could be doing other, more enjoyable things. They are individuals who accompany you to healing masses, and support you every step of the way, even though they think you're cuckoo. They are the ones who bring you food when you are too tired to prepare a meal yourself. Friends give, and give, and give, without taking in return. They are rare, and they are to be cherished. Let their dedication to you light a fire in your belly. My friends inspire me to persevere, because I know they are rooting for me with all their hearts. If I succeed, then they will succeed. If I fail, well, it's a moot point—I won't fail.

My son, Nico

Even when despair was getting the best of me a few years back, Nico still managed to give me tremendous joy. I shudder to think what condition I would be in today if it weren't for him. Nonetheless, even though I was outwardly happy when we were together, I was still a broken man on the inside. My whole outlook on life was still bleak. And when we weren't together, I was definitely not in a good state. I guess you could say that back then, Nico inspired me enough to keep breathing.

Okay, you can put the violin away, because when I got my head together and saw the truth, my outlook improved. Right now, Nico inspires me to do much more than just breathe. And that's the whole point of having a strategy against despair—we don't want to just survive it, we want to rise above it! But in order to overcome my grief, I had to change my mindset. Firstly, I asked myself a few questions. How do I want my son to see his father handle great adversity—with courage, strength and optimism, or like a weak, beaten-down pup? Do I want him to feel sad because his dad is always down in the dumps? And how about the reverse? How would I want *him* to face adversity? Wouldn't it give me great comfort to know that he is facing his hardship with a confident smile on his face, rather than with tears in his eyes? I see it this way. If I needed to, I would die a thousand deaths to spare my son from suffering. But that has not been asked of me. Instead, all I need to do to prevent his suffering is to be strong for him. I think I can handle that.

Consider the example of Todd Beamer, one of the September 11, 2001 heroes, whose words "let's roll" have inspired an entire country. He left behind a wife and three kids, who have suffered immensely at his loss. But his bravery and heroism have provided his family with a permanent comfort that nothing else could compare to. If the Beamer children were left with the image of their dad being desperate and afraid during his last moments, they might never recover from his death. But I guarantee, the fact that he was strong and resolved gives them the inner peace to carry on. That kind of gift is truly priceless. If my strength can comfort my son even a fraction as much as that, I would feel very fortunate.

I love my son dearly, and he inspires me to be the best father, and the best man, that I can be. But having a chronic and debilitating illness makes it very challenging to keep despair at bay. As you can imagine, there are times when I start to feel sorry for myself—without whining of course. When this happens, I focus on one particular thought, and without fail, the self-pity disappears. It's truly my secret weapon against despair. I consider the idea that my family may have some sort of quota for illness. I imagine that I've been given the choice of accepting my disease, and fulfilling the quota, or refusing it, and allowing my son to be vulnerable. The choice is simple; I will gladly accept any burden to spare my son. Seeing things in this light makes me feel so grateful to God that it's me who is ill, and not Nico. The funny thing is, I am not referring to a resigned, I-have-no-choice, sort of gratefulness. It is definitely a happy, skip-down-the-block, sort of gratefulness. I always pray to God that if he has any more "challenges" for my family, let them come my way. I can take whatever he's got.

Building your support network

I am of the view that one can never have too many supportive people in his corner. That's why it's important to build a support network, especially if supportive family and friends are scarce. Yet again, this requires opening up to others. But where do we find people to open up to? Almost everywhere you look, you can find supportive folks. Whether it's in your Book-of-the-Month Club, the health club, or the local PTA, there are always people who are dealing with circumstances similar to your own. I believe, however, that the most fruitful way to begin building your support system is by attending a church and/or support group.

Support groups

Unfortunately, I think there is a stigma attached to anything labeled as a support group because of the view that they are somehow only suitable for the weak and pathetic. Don't buy into this nonsense! These groups are not whining sessions, but rather discussions amongst people with the same experiences. Talking with people, who oftentimes are the only ones that truly understand you, can be as important to your support system as your loved ones. There is a plethora of support groups available for almost every illness or problem imaginable, so it shouldn't be too hard to find one near you.

If, however, you are uncomfortable with face-to-face meetings, there is also an abundance of web forums and support groups on the Internet. Most of these consist of message boards, and occasionally live chat rooms. These venues allow people to constantly connect with each other without regard to distance or time. This is an excellent way to gain knowledge, receive advice, and prevent feeling isolated.

Church

Up until a few months ago, I thought going to church was unnecessary because one can pray anywhere. I now think that going to church—the right one for you —can have great value. Recently, I have been attending a church service that provides uplifting music, a positive atmosphere, and sermons that address modern-day issues. But the real reason I go is to connect with others who are all striving towards a common goal. In doing so, I always return home invigorated.

Hopefully, you can find a church service that heartens and energizes you just as I have. Then, gradually you will find friends that will support you, and even carry you, through life's toughest challenges. Maybe you could even return the favor as well.

You are your own source

I have learned over the years that no matter how wonderful, or how supportive our loved ones are, sometimes we can feel alone in this world. And at times we have to succeed as individuals. As magical as it is to be loved and cared for, occasionally we need to feel whole, independent of anything external.

So thinking in that vein, I often ask myself, "What kind of man do I want to be?" It has been said that, "Circumstances do not make a man, they reveal him." Pondering this universal assertion, held by countless philosophers, can prompt one to self-evaluate. Every once in a while, try asking yourself, "Can I be proud of who I am revealing?" In this context, I am referring to what is revealed to yourself, not to others. If you are proud of what you uncover, you're in good shape. If not, then set out to be the person you will be proud of.

What my circumstances have revealed to me is that I am a strong person—something that I have always aspired to be. However, I'm not so sure I grasped what that truly meant, until recently. I know I'm beating a dead horse with this example, but when I used to lift obnoxious amounts of weight in the gym, I felt very powerful. What a rush! This intense feeling is what inspired me to continue such a nutty activity. In retrospect, this fleeting air of power was so minuscule compared to how invincible I feel when I realize: ***Parkinson's can't beat me!***

Inspire others

Feeling good about yourself is far more important than what others may think of you. Some people will sing your praises, while others may ridicule you. Either way, it doesn't change a thing. The exception, however, is if you make a positive impact on someone's life. If the way you handle adversity inspires others to overcome their own obstacles, you will be that much more driven to persevere. Essentially, *being* an inspiration, can in turn, *be* an inspiration. Every person that copes with life just a little bit better because of my example, serves to fortify my determination.

I know that I am not the only one who finds inspiration by inspiring others. Anna proved that to me. When I met her, she was clinically obese, weighing 285 pounds. Her appearance and lack of energy made her deeply depressed. Dealing with the constant pain in her foot, hip, and back certainly did not help matters.

Her problems began in her home country of Ecuador a few years earlier when she was introduced to a so-called Doctor. This quack told her that her back problems, which were minor at the time, could be corrected by "fixing" her flat feet. Somehow, she was convinced into undergoing a procedure that involved removing part of her hip-bone and grafting it onto her foot. I presume you can imagine how things progressed from there.

Due to this medical fiasco, she became very sedentary, and subsequently gained 145 pounds over the next few years. So when I met her, I tried to motivate her to lose weight and get healthy. Initially, I was unsuccessful. She kept insisting that she was a lost cause. So I thought if she wouldn't try to help herself, she might consider helping someone else.

That someone was an overweight, diabetic lady that I was helping lose weight. She was very hard to motivate, so I figured if Anna set an example, it would inspire her. After assuring Anna it would be a one-time deal, I trained the two women simultaneously. Naturally, they learned a lot about each other during the session. Inspired by Anna's courage and determination, my client was visibly filled with a new spirit. My plan had worked!

Afterwards, I thanked Anna for doing this good deed. When I saw her face gleaming with pride, I realized the sheer genius of my plan. Anna was there only to help, yet she was the true beneficiary. As we parted ways, she said confidently, "I could really do this thing." Now, I'm happy to say that after losing 90 pounds, and feeling healthy, she's still doing her thing.

In order to inspire people, you must be available to them. If your experience can benefit others, in any way, you should share it with as many people as possible. This is where your support network comes into play again. Churches and support groups are filled with people searching for comfort and inspiration. Share your struggles with them to show them they're not alone, and be sure to share your triumphs as well. Even your smallest victories will offer others hope.

As I mentioned previously, web forums on the Internet can be a big part of your support system. They can also be a great place to inspire a large number of people. Maybe there is a bit of information or advice you have to offer. Perhaps you want to share an inspirational poem or book that you have read. If you do have something positive or beneficial to share, there are many people out there that will be very grateful to hear it.

Helping others

It's no great revelation—helping others can be one of the most powerful sources of inspiration. The examples of inspirational people are infinite: The mother of a boy, who was killed by a drunk driver, starting an organization to stop drunk driving; the father of an abducted and murdered boy starting a television show to track down criminals; a man with Parkinson's Disease working tirelessly to raise money and awareness. These are all very special individuals, and their exceptional efforts should be lauded. But some of us don't have the wherewithal or the energy to help in this fashion. So if you can't help others by giving money, or time, or energy, give them a model of strength and courage to learn from.

Don't underestimate the significance of subtle gifts such as these. To some, the little things can make all the difference in the world. A Hasidic teaching tale, which I found in *How to Want What you Have*, by Timothy Miller, exemplifies this notion, and illustrates the universal benefit of giving to others:

> *A rabbi asked the Lord about Heaven and Hell. "I will show you Hell," said the Lord, and he led the rabbi to a round table. The people sitting there were desperately hungry, which was odd, because in the middle of the table there was a very large pot of stew. The smell of the stew was delicious and made the rabbi's mouth water. The people around the table held spoons with very long handles. The people knew that it was just possible to reach the pot and take a spoonful of the stew, but because the spoon handles were longer than a person's arm, the people could not get the food to their mouths. The rabbi saw that their*

> *suffering was terrible. The Lord said, "Now you may see Heaven." They went into another room, much like the first. They saw a similar big, round table, a similar pot of stew, and, as before, the people held similar long-handled spoons. But in Heaven they were well nourished. Their laughter and smiles clearly indicated they were happy. Seeing the rabbi's perplexity, the Lord said, "It is simple, but it requires a certain skill. They have learned to feed each other."*

Feed another, and you shall be nourished. What a great concept! Likewise, inspire others, and you shall be inspired. Give whatever you can to others, and you shall receive. As the Lord said in this parable, it does take a certain skill to grasp the fact that life is about more than just "me."

I never quite appreciated the depth of this concept until I became a father. A particularly poignant event that encapsulates this notion for me occurred while eating lunch with my son. We were at a casual restaurant that we frequented very often, so Nico was his usual boisterous self, flirting with all the waitresses and being a regular clown. Towards the end of our stay, my son was eating ice cream, while I was still finishing my meal. Of course, when it was my turn to have ice cream, he wanted mine too. Even though I normally try to teach him that he can't have everything, I gave it to him, nonetheless. Upon seeing this, our waitress looked at me disapprovingly and said, "Oh come now. You need to enjoy yourself once in a while too, ya know." After mulling over her comment for a brief moment, I replied, "You're right—that's exactly why I gave him the ice cream." She couldn't fathom the fact that watching the joy on my son's face as he appreciated the ice cream was infinitely more pleasurable than eating it myself. Sure, giving is an honorable thing to do in any context. But what many of us miss is that more often than not, the reward comes back to us tenfold.

In the previous chapter, I mentioned that my cousin Vincent was in need of help to cope with his divorce. So like a good cousin, I asked for *his* help instead. I suggested that he offer free Arts & Crafts lessons to the children at the hospital near his art gallery. This was a great opportunity for him to do something kind, and at the same time introduce his new gallery to the community. I hoped, however, that this good deed would have a more profound impact on all our lives.

And it did. The lessons offered the kids a brief respite from their struggles with the various health problems each of them faced. I gained many things from the experience, not least of which was a new appreciation for living in the moment. Despite unimaginable circumstances, these kids had the wisdom to enjoy every minute they had to the fullest. Last, but not least, the courage with which our young friends faced their hardships moved my cousin to an extent that I did not anticipate. Their example filled him with vigor and strength, which he used to face his own turmoil. Vinny gave a little, but wound up getting much, much more – the inspiration to defy despair.

Philosophy

I've spouted off enough about the importance of reading diverse philosophies and learning various techniques to cope with despair. Different ideas obviously appeal to different people. When you find something that strikes a chord within you, set it aside, and refer to it often. The writings of Wayne Dyer, Deepak Chopra, Tony Robbins and Allan Kardec, consistently inspire me to improve my way of thinking. As you can tell, I personally benefit more from our modern day philosophers, who relate better to modern day problems and values. For those interested in real-life inspirational stories, *Chicken Soup for the Unsinkable Soul*, by Jack Canfield, Mark Victor Hansen, and Heather McNamara, is chock-full of them.

The stories which remind me that great courage usually comes from ordinary people inspire me the most. Courage or inner strength is not a birthright, nor is it a matter of genetics—it's a matter of choice. Courage is not beyond the reach of anyone. Even a coward can become courageous from one second to the next. I have seen firsthand, how that type of mental strength can develop instantaneously. My mother used to cry twenty-four hours a day after she and my father separated many years ago. She was an emotional wreck. But one day, as if she flipped on a switch, she transformed. She was suddenly content, and solid as a rock. I guess she finally had enough. All of us have within us, this capacity; the remarkable ability to choose courage, and refuse to be a victim any longer.

Anybody, at anytime, can make the decision to be as powerful as they want to be. Search your heart. You know this to be true. You possess this power deep within you. Just acknowledging it will bring you that much closer to being able to harness it. Furthermore, simply realizing that you have this capacity, in and of itself, can be empowering. But then you need to take the next step—make the choice to let your power out.

Do you still doubt that we all possess this power? Do you still think that only people with the "hero gene" can be courageous? If so, you need to reflect a little more. Take a second to think of an example in your life, in which a weakened person suddenly chose to dig deep within, to find great power and courage. Perhaps you know of someone who was abused in a relationship, and finally took a stand. Or maybe you know of a lifetime drug user who turned his life around with one inexorable choice. Then of course, there are the more rare, Clark Kent-to-Superman stories.

The most striking example of instant courage and power that I've ever come across, can be found in *Chicken Soup for the Unsinkable Soul*, by Jack Canfield, et al. In the book, the authors recount a story that took place during the Vietnam war. It occurred in a little Vietnamese village, where an orphanage run by missionaries was accidentally hit by a mortar blast. Several people were killed and many were wounded. An American medical unit arrived on the scene and tended to the wounded. In the most critical condition was an eight year old girl. Without an immediate blood transfusion, she would die. But none of the American staff had the correct blood type. However, several of the uninjured orphans did. Despite a language barrier, the Americans managed to ask for volunteers to give blood. Only the trembling hand of one little boy ascended in the air. He was tentative, but willing. While the boy, named Heng , was giving blood, he started sobbing. The American nurse repeatedly asked if he was in pain, but he kept saying, "no." Nevertheless, Heng kept crying. By then, a Vietnamese nurse arrived and asked him what exactly was wrong. The fact was, the boy misunderstood what was going on. He thought he was asked to give *all* his blood, so that the girl could live. Puzzled, the nurse asked Heng why he would volunteer for such a thing. "Because she's my friend," he said meekly.

From one second to the next, this boy went from a frightened little child to a valiant hero with inestimable inner strength. No one forced him to raise his hand that day—he chose to.

Instant Inspiration

Music and/or gestures

Music has also been a great source of inspiration for me. Granted, songs provide more of a short term boost, but they are helpful nonetheless. That's especially true for me when I'm feeling lethargic, and well, sort of "blah." Sometimes to perk myself up, I crank up some Rock-n-Roll, and groove to a guy wailing on his guitar—the louder, the better. It's like an instant shot of adrenaline. During the intense parts, I usually raise my fist in the air, or run around with both arms up like I just won the Boston Marathon. I find this to be very invigorating, especially when my son joins in on the fun. I realize that this may sound a little hoakey, but it makes me feel good, so sue me. Believe it or not, I have science on my side on this one. Simple gestures like raising your fist in the air—as if to signify that you're defying despair—can release positive hormones. And hey, I'm all for that. Subtle expressions like smiling can produce similar results. That's one reason I enjoy watching a lot of stand-up comedy on television. What's really amazing is that even a fake smile releases positive hormones. So fake it if you have to.....um, just the smile I mean.

Music can be powerful on so many levels, from the melody to the words. But also, music helps us remember. Young children use songs to remember things like the alphabet, days of the week, and the like. As for adults, a song can instantly take us back to an experience twenty years in the past. It can allow us to, in a way, relive the experience. Our response to songs is comparable to our sense of smell in that they both have great memories. So if there are any songs that made you feel good in the past, then go ahead and break out those 45's if you have to. They might just make you feel good all over again.

Mantras

A mantra is a word or phrase repeated over and over again to produce a certain effect. A simple example, in which a mantra is used to produce an immediate affect, involves public speaking. In order to calm down before giving a speech, a nervous person might repeat the phrase, "The people in the audience are all my friends. They are pulling for me." This is also referred to as self-talk. Some mantras, in the form of proverbs, don't necessarily have to be repeated. Most useful are phrases that are personally significant, and put things in focus quickly. One that works for me comes from Confucius: "Great men are always themselves, wherever they are"

Many psychologists suggest using mantras in the form of affirmations, which are basically positive statements about one's self. These are intended for more of a long-term benefit, but they can quickly inspire you just the same. Affirmations consist of statements similar to these: "I am strong, I am healthy, I am complete;" "I continue to become better every day;" and "I am worthy of being happy." They should also be repeated many times, because as Aristotle once said, "We are what we repeatedly do." Affirmations are most effective when they are spoken aloud, which appeals to our sense of hearing. The reason being that, what we experience with our senses helps form our mind's view of reality. Hence, if we "experience" something enough—in this case, in the form of hearing it repeatedly—we will start to believe it. Once we believe it, our mind tries to make reality conform to our belief. And unless you skipped Chapter Seven, you know how powerful the human mind can be.

Our senses can be so influential that they can actually make our bodies react in a way that is completely inconsistent with reality. Have you ever taken a virtual roller coaster ride at a 3D movie theater, or at a theme park? If so, you know that no matter how hard you try to remind yourself that in fact you are not moving, your body reacts like it's bobbing and weaving. I know that when I experienced a similar ride at Universal Studios, I actually became nauseated. My sense of sight formed my reality, and apparently my stomach's as well.

Psychologists also recommend standing in front of a mirror while saying your affirmations. This way, the experience not only entails hearing the affirmation, but seeing yourself as the object of it, as well. I personally feel silly staring at myself in the mirror. Honestly, I feel a bit silly talking to myself too. But since I really believe in the efficacy of these techniques, I found a way around my hang-ups. Instead of monotonously reiterating the same set of words like a broken record, I sing my affirmations.

I utilize a variety of different affirmations to inspire me

on a daily basis. When I get up in the morning, I open up the window shades, and sing the chorus from, *It's a Great Day to be Alive*, by Travis Tritt: "And it's a great day to be alive, you know the sun's still shining when I close my eyes. It's a hard time in the neighborhood, so why can't every day be just this good." Then he punctuates the verse with a howl, so what the heck, so do I: "Ah-oooh!" And what about standing in front of the mirror, you ask? Well, I say or sing my affirmations while I'm brushing my teeth or shaving, and sometimes in front of my full-length mirror as I am getting dressed. This allays my feelings of silliness, because I technically have an "excuse" to be in front of the mirror. And on occasion, when I'm feeling extra feisty, I flex my tiny muscles and yelp, "Damn, I'm good-looking!"

Realizations

Now we are going to change gears. In the first half of this chapter, we explored sources of inspiration that don't require too much introspection or understanding. The desire to be strong for your son, or the rewards of helping others are relatively simple ideas to grasp. However, in the following section, the use of our thinking caps is required. Pull up your boot straps, because we're going a little deeper. Don't worry, though. Discussions on Oedipal complexes or penis envy are not part of our future. We're not going that deep.

Entitlement

I bet you've heard it a million times: "I deserve more than this." "I'm entitled to be happy like every one else." Nonsense! First of all, *not* every one else is happy. Secondly, you are entitled to absolutely nothing. When it comes right down to it, none of us were even entitled to be conceived. We were all fortunate just to be born. Consider everything after that as gravy. None of us are entitled to avoid pain, either; not the Queen of England, not the Pope, and not Humpty Dumpty. Nobody. Once we fully accept this fact, it will be easier to appreciate the good things in our lives, and easier to deal with the hardships.

Whenever I start thinking that I deserve to have a healthy body, I think of my childhood friend who died in a car accident sixteen years ago. This guy was the most competitive and most athletic person that I ever met. Incidentally, he is the one who taught me how to play baseball at a very early age. Besides being a great guy, he was very handsome, and extremely hard-working. What I'm trying to say is, he had it all. At twenty-one years old, he fell madly in love, and got engaged.

But right before his next birthday, his promising life was extinguished. Wasn't he entitled to more than he got? At least I've been afforded the opportunity to continue living, and to continue fighting. My friend was not. Knowing how he was, I'm certain he would have overcome any obstacle, if only he had been given the chance. I have been given that chance. Thinking of him makes me appreciate all the blessings and opportunities in my life. I guess my childhood buddy is still coaching me today, just as he always did in the past.

Responsibility

Once we accept that we are not entitled to anything, we must take some responsibility for our particular situations. However, many of us do not do so because it is far easier to play the victim. Being the victim requires nothing, besides the willingness to accept pity. Plus, being a victim provides a built-in excuse for one's failures and short-comings. They could just blame everything on whatever their particular hardship may be. But having courage means owning up to your actions, without making excuses, and still dealing with the disappointments of failure. I saw a quote from Erica Jong in the book *Courage*, by Sandra Ford Walston, that conveys the same idea. "Take your life in your own hands and what happens? A terrible thing: no one to blame."

Place blame: That's exactly what most of us do when something bad happens to us, isn't it? A few years ago, I blamed every single thing that went wrong in my life on my condition. If I could have blamed Parkinson's Disease for global warming, I would have. It's instinctual to want to find a culprit. And over time, we have learned to believe that finding one will make us feel better; it doesn't. It simply allows us to feel that our grief is justified. In essence, finding a scapegoat for our problems gives us an excuse to stay miserable.

There is some interesting data that supports this idea. In *How to Want What You Have*, by Timothy Miller, the author cites several studies that compared "people whose lives were disrupted by technological disasters, like explosions, or chemical spills, with people whose lives were similarly disrupted by natural disasters such as earthquakes, floods, and hurricanes. The victims of the technological disasters recover from their physical injuries much more slowly, suffer far more pain during the period of recovery, and are far more likely to develop serious psychological problems than the victims of the natural disasters." Why is this so? According to Mr. Miller, it's because with respect to the natural disasters, there is no one to blame. So the victims focus their energies on recovery. On the other hand, the victims of the technological disasters are too busy looking for a culprit to devote much attention to recovering. They're caught up in a Catch 22: I'm suffering, and you're to blame; you're to blame, so I continue to suffer. I guess the moral of the story is: Placing blame for your hardships will not empower you to overcome them, it will only weaken you enough to succumb to them.

Conditioning

We have all been conditioned, in one form or another, to think a certain way. Obviously, family, culture, religion, and relationships, play a huge part in forming our belief systems. Since at times, some of these influences can have a negative impact on us, not all of our beliefs are healthy ones, to say the least. Several years ago, I had a spoiled, very wealthy client, who constantly complained about how unhappy she was. Most of her displeasure was centered around her disdain for her husband, and the lack of love in her life. Despite accumulating a superfluous amount of material things, she was still unhappy. So one day, for laughs, I posed a silly question to her. I asked her if she would rather be happy, living with the man of her dreams in a one bedroom apartment, or be miserable and wealthy. Without hesitation or sarcasm, she said, "wealthy." I assume she was too embarrassed to include the "miserable" part in her response. I don't know why, but as ludicrous as it was, I expected that answer. This goes to show how deeply some ideas are ingrained; and how destructive they can be.

Much of our conditioning develops in early childhood. In my case, I was conditioned to believe that being a man meant being physically strong; strong enough to work fourteen hour days like my father did all his life, and strong enough to protect the family. Furthermore, I was always praised for my athletic abilities, and later on for my big "muscles." Other qualities I possessed never seemed to yield quite the same approval. Thus, my main source of self-esteem was derived from my physical prowess. I guess it's no accident that I became a personal trainer.

So when an illness comes along to strip you of everything that purportedly makes you a man, what is left? Well, in these circumstances, all that remained was a very empty human being. That is, of course, until I accepted the fact that there is much more to being a man than I thought. But before I could come to that realization, I had to find the proper perspective.

Perspective

Coping with Parkinson's was especially difficult for me, because I expected very specific things out of life. I always wanted to be a certain type of man, with a certain type of lifestyle. And my infirmity was flying in the face of those wishes. Having rigid expectations can definitely affect one's perspective regarding how good, or how bad, a situation really is. One of my own experiences serves as, I think, an amusing example of this.

Several years ago, I was eating dinner at home with my girlfriend, and she handed me a glass of Coke to go with my meal. I took a gulp and immediately spit it back in the glass, as if it were poison. "Ehh, that Coke is disgusting," I growled. To my surprise, my displeasure was greeted with a chuckle. "It's not Coke, it's grape juice," she said, "and you love grape juice!" Within seconds, my constipated face disappeared, as my taste buds began to recognize the pleasant taste of the juice. The point is, if you have narrow expectations—I expected Coke, and only Coke—almost anything else will leave you dissatisfied. I found it difficult to cope with my condition, because I was locked into the belief that there was only one way to be happy. Now that I have a different perspective, I'm not missing out on all the other pleasant "tastes" life has to offer.

Of course, I realize that Parkinson's Disease sure as heck ain't no grape juice. And that's exactly the point. It was easy to change my perspective with the grape juice. It was automatic. With regard to coping with illness or despair, however, a lot of introspection and effort is required.

This is where the probing questions come into play again. One day, I thought to myself, "What have I gained from getting Parkinson's?" The answers were surprisingly plentiful and astonishingly profound. On the surface, it was easy to see. I had become more compassionate, more sensitive, more appreciative, and more understanding. That was all very nice, but it just wasn't enough to start wishing Parkinson's Disease on family and friends. As I continued to ponder, I realized that if it weren't for my illness, I would have continued to work seven days a week at very inconvenient hours. That would have meant not being the first person to see my son crawl—I even captured it on video! Nor would I have been the first person to see him walk. If I didn't get Parkinson's, I would have missed out on the special bond we shared through our daily rituals of diaper changing, bathing, and constant playing. It would have meant spending much less time with my son during his most important years. In short, it would have meant missing out on everything that I cherish in my life. So, if I had a choice between missing out on all these things or getting Parkinson's Disease? You got it—I'll take the Parkinson's *every time!*

By changing my perspective, it was much easier to accept things as they were. So I began examining all my narrow, negative thoughts about my condition. One thought that always caused me great pain was the negative impact my illness would have on my son. I would constantly lament over thoughts such as: "Poor Nico has to deal with a dad who can't do certain father-son things; Poor Nico has to be patient while I struggle to dress him; or Poor Nico has to see his father weak and fragile." But in reality, I know now that he has gained far more than he has lost. In addition to having a special bond with me, he is learning patience, compassion, teamwork, and a whole host of other virtues. Eventually, he will be mentally strong, and better equipped to overcome adversity. Hopefully, he will also be appreciative of the gifts we are all given, especially our health. Now that I see the truth, I no longer fear being his source of embarrassment, but instead aspire to be his source of inspiration.

I want to share with you a proverb on the importance of searching for perspective. It comes from the *Art of Happiness*, by the Dalai Lama and Howard Cutler. I find it not only profound, but hilarious as well:

> *Once there was a disciple of a Greek philosopher who was commanded by his Master for three years to give money to*

everyone who insulted him. When this period of trial was over the Master said to him, "Now you can go to Athens and learn Wisdom." When the disciple was entering Athens, he met a certain wise man who sat at the gate insulting everybody who came and went. He also insulted the disciple, who burst out laughing. "Why do you laugh when I insult you?" said the wise man. "Because," said the disciple, "for three years I have been paying for this kind of thing and now you give it to me for nothing." "Enter the city," said the wise man, "it is all yours...."

Wisdom allows us to see things from the correct perspective. And this wisdom can inspire us to accomplish great things, and overcome great obstacles. Whenever I start to feel burdened by my illness, or anything in general, I read the words of Marcus Aurelius, philosopher and Roman Emperor: "If you are distressed by anything external, the pain is not due to the thing itself but to your own estimate of it; and this you have the power to revoke at any moment."

Wisdom of the Chinese

In the Chinese language, the character for crisis is a combination of the ones for danger and opportunity. This reflects the perspective that crisis can allow people the opportunity to improve their lives. According to Paul Pearsall, author of the *Beethoven Factor*, there is a new field of psychology called positive psychology which has discovered that "those who have known the worst of life often learned how to find the best out of living." Dr. Pearsall refers to this phenomenon as the "art of thriving" through adversity. He contends that most people live rather empty lives –

until a crisis occurs. That's when they learn how to get the most out of life. A story my father once told me certainly supports Pearsall's assertion.

My father came to this country from Italy in 1954. He found work quickly because he was a skilled welder and carpenter. Lacking any such skills, his friend Aldo was lucky to get a job in the stock room where my father worked. His lack of skills notwithstanding, Aldo was a tireless worker with an impeccable record of speed and efficiency. But when it was discovered that he was illiterate, he was fired after being on the job for over a year. Willing to take a pay cut, Aldo pleaded for his job, but his manager glibly blamed company policy for the decision.

Aldo had a wife and child, and needed a job desperately in order to put food on the table. Unfortunately, no one would hire him. With nothing to lose, he borrowed a few hundred dollars from sympathetic co-workers, and rented a small, dilapidated pizzeria. He fixed the place up, and worked as hard as he always had to provide for his family.

Approximately two years later, he returned to his former place of employment—in a limousine! With a bottle of Champaign in his hand, he strolled into his former boss's office to thank him. After all, if it weren't for him, Aldo would still be toiling in the stock room, barely surviving. Instead, he was the millionaire owner of three flourishing pizzerias. We can all learn from Aldo's example. Instead of falling back on excuses for his hardships, he found the opportunity to thrive in spite of them.

Pain vs. pleasure

Sometimes, we must face obstacles that are grueling,

painful, and frightening. And very often, in these situations, it is very difficult to find a perspective that comforts us. A great practical technique, described by Tony Robbins as "Pain versus pleasure," can be an enormous help in this regard. Mr. Robbins contends that humans are driven primarily by the instinct of avoiding pain and seeking pleasure. Many of our behaviors are based on this instinct. Therefore, we assign value judgments to our actions according to what we think is painful or pleasurable. We associate touching a hot iron with pain, so we avoid that particular activity. Many people associate money with the pleasure of material things, so they are drawn to activities such as working hard, pursuing lucrative professions, and even stealing. Although there are always exceptions, these examples represent obvious choices, for the most part.

Most value judgments we make on a daily basis are more ambiguous, however. Take for instance, the person who wants to lose weight. When faced with the decision to eat a greasy cheeseburger, a number of different value judgments can be made. This person can view the cheeseburger as immediate pleasure for the taste buds, or as the pain of poor health, a low self-esteem, and a flabby body. From my experience with clients, I know the taste buds usually win. Most likely, that's because the person associates the cheeseburger as the pleasure, and looking in the mirror afterwards as the pain. But if the individual in our example has the foresight to accurately view the *cheeseburger*, and not the act of looking in the mirror, as the cause of the pain, he/she will stand half a chance.

One major blunder I made in dealing with my illness was totally abandoning everything I knew to be important to good health. Before Parkinson's, my whole life revolved around exercise and nutrition. But when my condition made exercising excruciating, and preparing healthy meals laborious, I avoided both. I avoided working out, not only because of the physical pain and fatigue that accompanied it, but also because it represented a painful fall from grace. It felt like I went from Rambo to Pee Wee Herman. And that hurt. As far as making healthy meals; well, I focused on the exhausting aspect of the preparation, instead of the salutary aspect of getting the proper nutrients.

By placing the wrong value judgment on exercise and nutrition, I was sacrificing my own health. And I, of all people, should have known better. I'm not suggesting that all of a sudden, this technique has made exercising easy for me. Frankly, when it's not impossible, it's plain hell. Hey, I caught myself—that's the wrong value judgment! Instead, I should say, my exercise routine is essential to staying strong, limber, and healthy, and is one weapon in my fight against Parkinson's. It represents the pleasure of still being able to lift up, and play with my son, and allows me to avoid the pain of being frail and useless.

If you need to accomplish something difficult, use the pain versus pleasure technique. But do so with the big picture in mind. Do you need to undergo intrusive tests? Do you need chemotherapy? Did your doctor instruct you to follow a strict diet? Are you too tired to exercise? Do you want to be strong enough to face your travails? You have the ability to do it. Find where the true happiness lies, and locate the real source of pain, and you'll find the power to do anything.

Why me?

In the history of mankind, no one has ever gotten a response to this question. So why do we continue asking it? Even though it's an utterly useless endeavor, we all fall victim to this syndrome at one time or another. Isn't it curious, though, that we pose that question only when things don't go our way? I never once asked, "Oh why, oh why was Nico born so healthy, or why was I born in the United States, instead of some impoverished country?" Nor did I ever question the sweet smell of a rose, or the warmth of the sun on my skin. No, I merely accepted these treasures of nature without question. But when I encountered something that didn't smell so sweet, I immediately began looking for justification.

My illness made me feel unfairly singled out, which happens to be a common feeling amongst people who face tragedy. The fact that Parkinson's is so rare in young people exacerbated the situation. It really irked me that the odds of a twenty-five year old getting Parkinson's were about as good as someone getting hit by lightning—indoors! How could I be so unlucky? It never occurred to me, however, that I should be more concerned with the severity of my illness, not the rarity of it. Would I have been more at ease if I had something more common, like a fatal heart attack? I didn't look at it that way of course. Instead, I focused on the negative. My illness made me so self-absorbed that I felt like the only one in the world who was suffering. And no one had reason to feel bad but me.

Nothing proves this last point more than when a close friend's dog died. She was genuinely heart broken, and needed a shoulder to cry on. Despite her tears, I had the audacity to say, "Give me a break. It's a dog; a dog for God's sake!" I was expressing my feelings honestly at the time. Unfortunately, I was also being an insensitive, self-absorbed, idiot. I was so closed off that I caused my friend even more pain. Fortunately, I'm sure she got over it rather quickly. And even though I feel badly for my past behavior, like her, I'm not too troubled by that particular incident anymore.

But there was another instance in which the implications of being so self-concerned were tragic. Several years ago, a member at the athletic club where I worked was referred to me for personal training. He was a sophisticated man in his forties, who spoke very little English. I had seen him around the club before, because he spent at least eight hours a day there, playing tennis, getting massages, and eating lunch and dinner. The reason he wanted personal training was that he hurt his wrist, and could no longer play tennis—his passion. Despite never having worked out before, he immediately wanted to schedule three hour appointments, five days a week! I told him that since Mr. Olympia didn't even train that much, the schedule he wanted was an impossibility. But he insisted that we could spend some of the time walking on the golf course or swimming.

Once I capitulated, we started our sessions immediately. I learned a lot about him, since we were spending fifteen hours a week together. He was extremely intelligent, wealthy, and generous. But he had no family; no wife, no children, no parents, and no siblings. Since he had recently come to this country, he had no friends either. Despite his good cheer, he was an immeasurably lonely man. One time he even confessed to me that all he ever wanted in life was to meet the woman of his dreams. He followed up by saying that he had finally given up on that idea.

Anyway, several weeks passed, during which time he would occasionally invite me to grab some lunch. I always declined. Then one week, he invited me three separate times to go to my choice of lunch or dinner. Once, he even called me at home to make the invitation. Although I was nice about it, I always turned him down. A few days later, he was dead. I couldn't believe my ears when I heard he had killed himself. Did I know he was going to kill himself? I had no clue. And that was the problem—I should have. I was too wrapped up in my own problems to recognize his blatant cries for help. I will carry around that guilt for the rest of my life.

It is painfully evident that I should've been more empathetic towards other people's pain. Not only could that have prevented their suffering, but it could have eased mine as well. Being self-absorbed and isolated only served to internalize my pain. I didn't accept that everyone has their own cross to bear; all of us suffer. There is great comfort in knowing that you're not alone. I realize that now. Looking at my illness as part of the human condition makes it much easier to deal with.

Yet, when life seems unfair, many of us will continue to muse upon the question that can only inspire one to scratch his head: "Why me?" We would benefit much more to ponder questions which inspire solutions. Unfortunately, without great effort, solutions are hard to come by. Therefore, it's much easier to dwell on the negative. In my days of despair, I could only focus on how life was being unfair to me. And maybe it was a little unfair. After all, I was a young man who made a life of being fit and healthy. I did not drink, do drugs or smoke. I didn't even drink coffee for crying out loud! In high school, my friends used to smoke pot on a daily basis, but I never partook. The main reason: I didn't want to destroy any brain cells! Then, on the other hand, you have the people who indulge in all of life's vices without the slightest of consequences. My attitude was that this just isn't the way things ought to be.

As you could guess, my perspective now is a lot different. I now realize that my healthy lifestyle was not in vain, because it prepared me for the challenges I now face. What condition would I be in today if I had lived a decadent lifestyle in the past? And more importantly, what condition will I be in five years from now if I don't continue being conscientious? Now these are useful questions to be asking. I prefer to leave the rhetorical questions to the English professors.

CHAPTER NINE
Tenacity

I once read that John Grisham's first manuscript was rejected over fifty times; the concept for Kentucky Fried Chicken was rejected over a hundred times; and Vanna White was turned down by countless modeling agencies, before being hired for the Wheel of Fortune. Almost all successful people have had to go through similar processes to achieve their goals. John Grisham, Kentucky Fried Chicken, and Vanna White are now household names for one reason—tenacity. Tenacity is defined as the quality of being very adhesive or sticky, and difficult to pull apart. The imagery of sticking to my goals and not letting go, no matter how hard Parkinson's may swing me around, is very powerful for me.

Being Relentless

Another word which can be interchanged with tenacity is perseverance. The ability to persevere through any failure or hardship is a vital part of defying despair. After all, to put it in terms of combat, some enemies will simply be stronger than you—at least in the beginning. But as the

Seventeenth Century English poet, H. Jackson Browne realized, superior strength can be overcome by unrelenting effort. He wrote: "In the confrontation between the stream and the rock, the stream always wins—not through strength, but by perseverance."

In order to persevere, however, one needs stamina. Physical stamina, for example, is not developed overnight. It gradually increases over time. As a personal trainer, I am particularly qualified to attest to that fact. When someone first starts an exercise program, he/she may become fatigued from a simple five minute walk on the treadmill. Many people are so discouraged that they quit, right there and then, because they think it's a lost cause. On the other hand, a person who sticks with the program may be able to run a marathon, one day. One day, not the next day.

Developing mental stamina is no different; it takes time. The key is to realize that at first, the struggle with despair will exhaust you, even before you have begun to fight. But in no way does this represent a lost cause, because invariably, your stamina will improve with each passing day. There is no doubt that eventually, with patience, commitment, and consistency, you will develop marathon-level mental stamina.

Patience

W.B. Prescott conveyed the importance of facing our struggles with patience when he said, "In any contest between power and patience, bet on patience." Since I always try to look to nature for examples, let's examine the pit-bull—the fiercest fighting dog in the world. Even though these modest-sized dogs rarely lose a fight, their great jaw strength has little to do with it. In fact, there are many breeds that greatly outmatch the pit-bull in size and strength. Nevertheless, the pit-bull will invariably defeat the strongest of opponents because he is unrelenting and tenacious. But most importantly, he prevails by being patient. His goal is to sustain his attack, while keeping the other dog at bay. All the while, he waits—actively, but nonetheless patiently—for his opportunity. Then, when his bigger adversary inevitably tires, he seizes that opportunity—game over.

Besides liking the occasional dog biscuit, I have a few other things in common with the pit-bull, including tenacity. Patience, however, has never been one of my strong suits. And I have had to struggle with this shortcoming in coping with my condition. Parkinson's has made sure to test my lack of patience on every front. Initially, accepting the fact that finding a cure for my illness could take twenty or thirty years was the biggest hurdle. Since I have no control over when that day will come, it is easier for me to be patient in this regard.

It has been a little harder being patient with regard to my own personal development, however. After making the commitment to fight despair, I expected to conquer it in a jiffy. Every time I would succumb to a moment of grief, I would get down on myself. "What's wrong with me?" I would lament, "I've read this self-help book three times, and I still feel like crap!" Well, as I've reiterated, there is no quick-fix in dealing with something like chronic illness. It takes a long time, and great pains to finally come to a point when you have some control. Recovering from a divorce or the death of a loved one can be quite a long process as well. After reading this book, you still may be despondent. After ten more books, and a year of introspection, you still may find it difficult to cope with your situation. But with patience, that moment will arrive. I promise.

That moment, whether it is in the form of enlightenment, or relief from despair, will certainly come. Until then, we must show the forbearance, and the strength of purpose to wait. Of course I mean actively waiting, not twiddling your thumbs and looking at your watch. And the simple reason we must wait is that there is no alternative. After all, no amount of impatience will hasten the arrival of your ultimate moment of relief. To keep this in perspective, I often refer to a quote from John Christiansen Morgenstern: "Consider the hour glass; there is nothing to be accomplished by rattling or shaking; you have to wait patiently until the sand, grain by grain, has run from one funnel into the other."

Forget the End, Focus on the Means

Perseverance is truly one of the most admirable traits one can possess. That is why we all love the character, Rocky Balboa. He was not smart, or fast, or very skilled for that matter. We loved him, nonetheless, because of one simple thing—he never gave up. In the original movie, Rocky was so outmatched by his opponent that getting trounced was a foregone conclusion. Although he knew he had absolutely no chance to win, he focused on achieving something that had never been done before; going the full fifteen rounds with Apollo Creed. And despite being brutally pummeled, he accomplished his goal.

In *Courage*, Harper Lee is quoted to say, "Real courage is when you know you're licked before you begin, but you begin anyway and see it through no matter what." If I had to give my son one phrase to live by, "never give up" would probably be at the top of the list.

The imagery of a boxer being beaten down, but never giving up, motivates me to persevere. But the reality is, being beaten down emotionally can sometimes be much harder to handle. That is why we admire people that keep plugging away no matter what. We all aspire to have the type of drive that propels someone to succeed, no matter how many times he/she has failed in the past. Failure doesn't seem to dissuade such tenacious individuals. And why should it, really? There are far worse things than failure. Nineteenth Century English novelist, George Eliot, expressed this sentiment so eloquently when he wrote, "Failure after long perseverance is much grander than never to have a striving good enough to be called a failure."

Look back at your life, and you'll see that he was right on point. What do you consider your biggest disappointments? Are any of these disappointments the result of trying too hard, and failing? Or was the problem that you didn't try hard enough? Or maybe even worse, you didn't try at all.

Let me use an example. I was at a bar with two average looking male friends of mine, and sitting across from us was a gorgeous woman. As the situation stood, she had all the control; the power to stand pat, the power to shoot anyone down, the power to toy with someone, or the power to respond positively. My buddies only had two possible options: Approach her and most likely get rejected, or do nothing and drool all night. One of them usually made an attempt in these situations and the other one always wimped out. And this night was no different.

The night ended as usual too—they both left alone. However, the one who never tries went home feeling defeated and somber. He probably even sulked for a few days. The poor sap has no control over his love life, and that night he did nothing to change that. Now at worst, my other friend may have felt a bit bummed out, but it didn't appear that way. Most likely he felt pretty good about himself. After all, he had some measure of control. He dictated how he would approach the woman, how he would follow up, and how he would handle her rejection. Who knows? Maybe next time he will say just the right thing to captivate his dream girl, and they'll live happily ever after. At least he continues to afford himself that possibility. In the meantime, he takes comfort in the fact that he is doing the best that he can do. Nothing can take that power away from him.

Don't dwell on the past

Just as focusing on the end result may not be the best way to persevere, especially when the goal is seemingly out of reach, dwelling on the past is equally unproductive. Individuals that constantly face failure—such as my friend at the bar—continue to persevere because they refuse to let the past dictate the present. When we feel bombarded by hardship after hardship, we must employ that same philosophy as well.

Did you ever have one of those days in which everything went terribly wrong? Odds are that by day's end, even the slightest annoyance was liable to set you off. That's because when problems continue to mount, it becomes harder and harder to get through the day without breaking at some point. The same holds true for our lives in general. Holding on to the problems of the past makes it increasingly difficult to persevere, until we eventually reach the breaking point.

Only recently have I realized just how important letting go of the past is when facing adversity. A few months ago I was rushed to the Emergency Room because of dizziness, disorientation, and severe chest pain. After two days in the hospital, the doctors figured a drug interaction was the cause of my symptoms. Then last month, I went back to the ER because of intense stomach pains that rendered me unable to stand. Apparently I developed an ulcer due to all the aspirin I was taking for a month-long headache. Last week I was in the ER again with intense pain and pressure in the head, ears, and jaw. The same stomach pain was still there also. At this point, the doctors suspect that I have a serious vascular condition on top of everything else.

During my latest hospital visit, I felt very discouraged and emotionally drained. As I was looking at the nurse drawing my blood, all I could think about was what a rough few months I had endured. But the reality was that at that moment, I was not dealing with anything that occurred in the past—those things were over. When I confronted my problem as a momentary one, and not the sum total of everything that occurred during the previous few months, I felt a renewed ability to cope.

I think approaching one's problems in this fashion is like approaching a game of Billiards. When a pool player takes the first shot, the balls scatter all over the table. He then has to assess all his options and take his best shot. After the shot, many of the balls are repositioned. To consider the previous positions would be useless. Therefore, he must approach each subsequent shot as a new challenge, reassess his options, and move on from there. Life is the same way, with each day bringing new challenges and demands. In order to persevere through life's toughest challenges, we must move forward by continuing to reassess, refocus, and recommit. The troubles of the past are gone, and the only way they can affect you is if you invite them back into the present.

Turn a Vice Into a Virtue

Obviously, dealing with a chronic illness requires a high level of tenacity or perseverance. Now I know that perseverance seems like a word used to describe the attributes of some mystical hero. It's not. We all have the power to persevere against any odds. If you don't believe me, let's examine the misfit relative of perseverance—obstinacy. Now even though we view obstinacy, or stubbornness, as being negative, isn't it essentially the same thing as perseverance? Very stubborn people stick to their guns no matter how wrong they are, and no matter how many people are against them. We all know far too many of these individuals, many of whom drive us absolutely nuts!

So why can't we put our pig-headedness to good use? Believe me, I have been accused of being inordinately stubborn in the past. And I have tried working on it—well, a little bit anyway. But I believe this attribute has served me well in my fight with Parkinson's. I may be a stubborn fool, but I'm not going to give in. Certainly not this time. Certainly not with my life on the line. I made a decision to defy my despair, and I'm sticking to it!

Even Great Men and Women Get Fatigued

It's important to understand that being tenacious doesn't mean never breaking down. Even the best of us falter. That's what the renowned philosopher, Friederich Neitzsche, meant when he said, "Even the greatest of men get fatigued." Pain, sorrow, and fatigue are all part of the human experience, so don't fight it. If you want to cry, then cry. If you need to wallow or break down, then do it. God, there have been so many times when I've sobbed like a baby, muttering to myself, "I don't want to deal with this anymore!" Fortunately, for the past couple of years, I have felt so strong that I haven't broken down at all. But this disease is merciless, and I know there is always that occasion of vulnerability. Consequently, I expect there will be occasions when I will break down crying and indulge in self-pity. And that's okay, because I know I will bounce back.

Giving in without giving up

Giving in to your fatigue and frustration in no way implies throwing in the towel. Give yourself the right to take a break from your problems, but do not quit. If you have a goal, keep moving towards it, especially if there is light at the end of the tunnel.

One of my friends, Kathy, started her own import/export business a few years ago. In order to obtain the necessary start-up capital, she took the risk of getting an equity loan on her house. She worked tirelessly on making the business viable, while continuing to work at her regular job. In addition, she still had to keep house for her and her son.

From the very beginning, Kathy struggled to keep the business afloat. After two years of pouring her own money into the company, it was still not generating cash flow. Consequently, her house was in foreclosure, her car was repossessed, and her utilities were even shut off. Wiped out financially, Kathy was on the verge of losing everything she had worked so hard for. Despite the dire straits, she was starting to develop potentially fruitful relationships with important contacts. But the stress of her world crumbling all around her was taking its toll. She felt that she had already given every ounce of effort she could muster—all to no avail. Giving up at that point was her way of facing reality.

On the other hand, I believed she still had some fight left in her. With her having so much vested in the business, and not having much more to lose, I refused to see her quit. Of course, the first task for her was to build a foundation of faith and inspiration. Since she always believed in herself, and adored her son who was her inspiration, she was ahead of the game. Convincing her that she had the "stuff" to persevere required a bit more effort.

I had her read much of the material contained in this chapter, but two simple sentences seemed to move her the most. The first one was a quote from Ralph Waldo Emerson: "The hero is no braver than the ordinary man, but he is braver five minutes longer." The other was this one-sentence story: There once was a man who swam 75% of the way to his destination, but he got tired so he swam back. Obviously, this guy should have continued forward, and that's exactly what Kathy did.

Today, she is still in business. I wish I could say that she is a millionaire, but it's only been a few months. As for now, she avoided foreclosure on her home, and the business is even starting to make money. Ultimately though, a sense of satisfaction is her greatest achievement, and will be a driving force behind her continued financial and personal success.

Take advantage of setbacks

Invariably, setbacks are followed by periods of progress and renewed strength. That was always the case for me in the past. Why is that? I surmise it's partly because this "breakdown" period is the only time when I got to rest. You see, someone who is dealing with Parkinson's, or a similar chronic illness, never gets to rest. Not only are the symptoms present twenty-four hours a day, seven days a week, but the consequences of the disease weigh heavy on the mind every moment of every day as well. So all my resources were constantly being used to cope with my condition. But during the times when I broke down, I totally let go; no coping, no fighting, just wallowing. And this brief respite from my responsibility to "hold it together," always left me refreshed and energized. Although I have heard it hundreds of times, the dictum, "Whatever doesn't kill you, makes you stronger," still rings true for me.

If we look to nature again, we will see how breaking down in order to build up stronger is a necessary process. Let's use the human body as an example. In order to make the muscles of the body bigger and stronger, we must damage them first. Bodybuilders accomplish this by lifting heavy weights, which causes micro-tears in the working muscle. The body responds by not only repairing the damage, but by synthesizing new muscle tissue to prepare for future trauma. So the next time you find yourself marveling at a bodybuilder's physique, appreciate the fact that his great size and strength are directly attributable to constant trauma and damage.

Wallowing like a champ

As I have said before, wallowing on occasion is perfectly normal, and can even be beneficial. But in *How to Want What you Have*, Timothy Miller takes it one step further by actually encouraging it. In certain circumstances, he will instruct his clients to immerse themselves in their feelings of fear and grief. I said previously that if you feel like wallowing, then wallow. Mr. Miller's view is, if you feel like wallowing, then wallow—with all your might.

He sites an example involving one of his patients, who was distraught over being investigated by the government for fraud and other crimes. His life was in a tumult. Dr. Miller suggested that he set aside an hour a day, and told him to "do nothing except feel as scared as you can possibly feel. If you feel you will go crazy, don't stop. If you think you might die, don't stop. If you cry, don't stop." According to the book, after about twenty minutes of this exercise, the patient's fear vanished. He was unable to feel scared after that, even when he tried. Once he realized that he wasn't going to spontaneously combust, his situation became tenable.

This is exactly what happened to me, when I decided to turn my life around at the moment of my deepest despair. As bad as I felt, I knew I wasn't going to die. Therefore, my only alternative to the pain of despair was to find a way to overcome it. A lot of tears may have fallen in the process, but I eventually found the way. And to think, it all started because I was a superb wallower. I guess that illustrates the importance of being true to your feelings. Don't be ashamed to breakdown. Instead, relish the opportunity to rest, and build up even stronger than before.

Worst case scenario

Another advantage to immersing yourself in your feelings of distress is that it forces you to think of the worst case scenario. Assessing the situation in this way will often make you realize that your dilemma isn't that grievous after all.

I have a friend named Savannah who was recently diagnosed with benign tumors on her ovaries. She was so scared and depressed that she neglected everything else in her life. Obviously, any health crisis can be frightening, especially when there are many unknowns. But Savannah was well-informed about her condition, so she knew what to expect. With this in mind, I tried to make her focus on the worst possible outcome.

In order to facilitate this process, I asked her some personal questions soon after she was diagnosed. Of course at first I told her how sorry I was, and that I would be there for her whenever she needed. Then the probing began. First, I asked her what the survival rate is, knowing that the answer would be nearly 100%. This may sound unnecessary to you, but the fear of death can be overwhelming, and even the slightest health problem can bring it to the surface. Focusing on the fact that you are not going to die can help diminish this fear. The questioning continued with, "God, how are you going to pay your bills if you can't work anymore?" Again, I knew her ability to work would not be affected. With every area that I covered, from her ability to enjoy sex to her ability to participate in sports, her answers pointed towards one truth—her life essentially would be the same as before. By the time we said our good-byes, Savannah showed no signs of fear at all.

I realize that many people are facing challenges that *will* substantially change their lives. Therefore, thinking of a worst-case scenario might appear to be depressing. But in any case, it's important to know exactly what you're up against. Maybe you're up against a huge challenge, in which case thinking of the worst possible outcome might not make you feel too much better. However, I believe most of the time our fears far exceed the reality of the situation. If this is the case, then you will at least be comforted by realizing that things aren't quite as horrific as you initially thought.

Daily Commitment

I suppose I haven't broken down lately because my illness does not weigh as heavily on my mind as it did in the past. I can directly attribute that to all the things I have learned over the past few years. But none of that enlightenment would mean a thing without committing myself daily to my goal. This entails reaffirming my beliefs, engaging in the activities that inspire and fortify my mind and body, and continually trying to improve myself. To do this, I find it essential to have a written routine that I follow every day. That's because I realize that if I start to neglect what got me here, my resolve will start to weaken.

I get creative too, every once in a while. In one instance, I jotted down an outline for a possible screenplay of my life. In it, I included several scenarios in which I was faced with unspeakable adversity. Then I digressed into thoughts of who would portray me in the movie, Brad Pitt or Tom Cruise. Of course I eventually decided that neither one of them was good-looking enough. When I returned to earth, I thought about how I would want my character to be portrayed in the movie. What qualities would I want him to display, when faced with his tribulations? I asked myself, "Do I display these qualities on a daily basis?" Of course, after I came up with the answers, I worked on my deficiencies. All right, I'll come clean—I was bored that day. But it was an interesting and beneficial endeavor nonetheless.

When I'm feeling especially lousy, particularly physically, an hourly commitment is necessary. That usually entails a simple prayer for strength, or an acknowledgment of the gifts in my life. This type of vigilance is necessary at times to keep despair at bay. There is no such thing as automatic pilot when you are dealing with a chronic condition.

Sometimes it can be frustrating, fighting the good fight, day in and day out, without that quick gratification. That's especially true in my case, where my disease is constantly progressing. The progressive nature of my illness sometimes makes it difficult to gauge the efficacy of my efforts. And worse yet are the days that I focus extra hard on feeling good, only to feel extra lousy. But in my heart, I know I can accomplish great things with sustained effort. This Taoist proverb helps me keep that in focus.

> *Act without contriving: work naturally, and taste the tasteless; magnify the small; increase the few, and reward bitterness with care. Seek the simple in the complex, and achieve greatness in small things. It is the way of nature that even difficult things are done with ease, and great acts*

made up of smaller deeds. The sage achieves greatness by small deeds multiplied.

Indeed, the small deeds done on a daily basis will ultimately lead to great things. I truly believe that. That's why I keep plugging away.

The Fight Itself Is Its Own Reward

The idea of fighting against a seemingly invincible foe until your very last breath is quite a romantic notion. In my case, I truly see no alternative, unless of course you consider misery to be a viable option. I'm no hero for persevering—I'm just fighting for my life. But what about those who voluntarily risk everything, solely for an ideal or a principle. Selfless people who will fight with their last breath for the benefit of others. There are countless examples of such courageous and persevering individuals. Mohandas Gandhi, Martin Luther King, and Nelson Mandela, all of whom never gave up their fight for freedom and justice, stand out in my mind.

These are all grand examples, but people of the same ilk are fighting similar battles all around us, everyday. Just think about all the people who tirelessly fight against things such as poverty, child abuse, and drug abuse. And what about doctors, like Dr. Abraham Lieberman of the National Parkinson's Foundation, who literally work eighteen hour days to help and comfort the sick and their families. All these individuals have a choice. And they choose to steadfastly fight for others—without personal gain. John Ruskin said, "The highest reward for a man's toil is not what he gets for it, but what he becomes by it." Well, if these great people willingly endure their toils without giving up, solely to help others, then I surely will not give up my fight either.

In our battles with despair, giving up on life is not righteous. Wasting any part of it is surely not righteous, either. In a spiritual sense, giving up, at any point, is wrong because God gave us life for a reason. Hypothetically, if you were definitely going to die next week, it would be unjust to give up the fight today. That's because if God really wanted you to give up today, he would have taken you today, instead of allowing you one more week of life. But in a more practical sense, wasting that last week of life may deprive you of something precious, whether it be reconciling with a loved one, sharing a special memory with someone, or a million other things you can think of.

Tenacious until that day

The phrase, "Live every day as if it were your last," has become so cliché that I think it has lost its significance. But think about it. What if tomorrow really was your last day? Would you spend it complaining? Would the fact that you were sick, or lonely, or unemployed, stop you from doing the things that you enjoy the most? Most likely, it wouldn't. And what if you had two days left? Would these so-called hardships stop you then? So I ask you this: Why do such things stop you now? If you have the power and tenacity to overcome adversity for one day, or ten days, or a hundred days, then you can eventually make it until your last day, whenever that may be.

PART III:

The Physical Challenge

Chapter Ten
The Miracle Of Exercise

Listening To Your Body

After what I consider my "period of discovery," I felt like I could eat nails. Without a doubt, this state of mind had a profoundly positive effect on my overall health. Along with this came an increase in my activity level and my ability to exercise. However, physical limitations still remained. Let's be realistic—Parkinson's Disease is not just something you can "walk off" like a sprained ankle or a Charlie horse. Sometimes, no matter how positive my frame of mind is, my body will just not do what I want it to do. Being so constrained was making it difficult to get fit.

Since I was not going to give up, I decided to employ a different, more flexible, approach to my workouts. When my muscles were too cramped or uncoordinated to perform a certain exercise, I would try a different one. When I was too fatigued to do my workout, I would choose a less taxing routine. When my stiff Parkinsonian muscles were too sore to workout, I would choose a stretching routine for that day. This "care-free" style of training was different than the regimented routine I had been accustomed to in the past, but I liked it—and it was working.

My strength, energy level, and mobility all improved very quickly because I was no longer fighting against my body. Instead, I was exercising within the parameters that it set for me. Even though these parameters were quite narrow at times, my goal was to exercise my body, or at least move it, as much as physically possible. At that point, working out was no longer solely about looking good in a tank shirt. What I came to realize was that looking good in bikini underwear was much more important. Oh yeah, the dramatic improvement in the quality of my life might be worth a mention as well.

Nature's Prescription

Wouldn't it be sublime if there was a single wonder-drug that could lengthen life-span, reduce the risk of heart disease, diabetes, and cancer, prevent osteoporosis, combat depression, enhance mood, and boost the immune system? Then as a bonus, throw in less body fat, more strength and stamina, and more energy. If it existed, this drug would be a bigger blockbuster than Viagra. Okay, maybe not Viagra, but it would be BIG nonetheless. Well, I am not a physician, but I am qualified to give you the prescription for this medical miracle—exercise!

Disease management & prevention

Without question, exercise is an essential part of preventing and managing illness. In fact, many health insurance companies offer their policy holders large incentives to exercise as a means of cutting health care costs. The

Chronic Disease Self-Management Program, developed by Stanford University Kaiser Permanente and the University of California, San Francisco recently conducted a study which supports the wisdom in this approach to health care.

In the study, 952 adults with either heart disease, lung disease, stroke, or arthritis were taught how to manage their illnesses through diet and exercise. The participants were randomized to the CDSMP group or the usual treatment group (controls.) Compared to the control group, the CDSMP group significantly improved their overall health status, increased their social activities, and had fewer hospitalizations. Overall savings in health care costs were $750.00 per participant over a 7 week period. The issue of health care costs is particularly relevant because a healthier you means more profits for the insurance companies. So you can be sure that if they are using their resources to encourage exercise, it is for good reason.

I think most people take it as a given that exercise improves overall health. But numerous studies have confirmed that exercise has specific therapeutic effects on various health problems, such as HIV, cancer, and diabetes. Even as I write, there is an ongoing study investigating the neuroprotective benefit of exercise on Parkinson's patients. Researchers now have reason to believe that regular exercise may slow down the disease's progression by somehow strengthening deteriorating brain cells. Preliminary results indicate an improvement in symptom relief as well.

Another recently completed study suggests that exercise may reduce or delay the deterioration of health associated with ALS. This neurological condition, commonly referred to as Lou Gehrig's Disease, progresses much faster than Parkinson's, and usually results in death within a few years. The clinical trial concluded that "relative to the control subjects, the participants in the exercise group demonstrated a smaller decrease in muscular strength, less pain, and a lower perceived deterioration of quality of life."

There is one recent finding that, despite never being studied in humans, has researchers of every neurological disease buzzing. Rats studied for a theoretical paper were exercised on one side of the body and not the other, and then after they were killed, their brains were examined. The side of the brain opposite the exercised limbs looked healthier than the side corresponding to the non-exercised limbs. Even though many studies in animals don't produce similar results in humans, this gives us one more reason to acknowledge the salutary effect of exercise.

I am confident that exercise has been the key to my success against Parkinson's. I am almost as confident that, properly done, it can help anybody with any condition. If you're sitting there, thinking that you are too "sick" to benefit from exercise, perhaps you should read Christopher Reeve's book, *Nothing is Impossible*. As you may know, Reeve is paralyzed from the neck down as a result of an equestrian accident in 1995. But recently, he has accomplished physical feats that have boggled the minds of doctors and scientists alike. As described in his book, Reeve has actually been developing the ability of voluntary movement—a feat that heretofore was considered impossible.

Needless to say, his accomplishments are of great interest to the medical community. Reeve's doctors have done numerous tests in an effort to find some explanations. After exhaustive research, they were left with one conclusion:

Reeve's intensive exercise regimen has been helping his body "regenerate," and develop new neural pathways. This superman can't hike, jog, or even walk, yet his exercise routine still puts us all to shame. Reading how Reeve endured hours of grueling exercise every day for almost a decade, just to be able to move his fingers and toes, puts many things in perspective. He is the epitome of strength and determination.

Depression

Irrespective of its obvious physical benefits, exercising just flat out feels good. I view it as nature's version of a "happy pill." Therefore, I believe that exercise is a must for those suffering from depression. Unlike most health issues, such as diabetes or cancer, depression is a condition that all of us can personally relate to. Virtually every one of us will feel seriously depressed at one point or another. But could you imagine feeling this way all the time? How horrible would it be to be perpetually depressed, no matter how ostensibly perfect your life was? Many people don't have to imagine it because they live it, every day. The inordinate amount of people in this country taking Prozac and other similar drugs speaks to the depth of the problem.

Exercise can benefit these individuals because it has been proven to enhance mood and increase life satisfaction. As a matter of fact, many psychiatrists prescribe it as a first line of defense against depression. I know this first-hand because over the years I have trained several people receiving professional therapy. And to each one of them, their daily workout was every bit as important as their medication. Again, the proof that exercise can enhance mood and help combat depression is uncontested.

So it follows that if exercise can benefit those with clinical depression, it can help the rest of us downtrodden as well. When I was eighteen years old, I developed this habit of running after every fight I had with my girlfriend. Why? Because it made me feel better. Maybe this is one instance where you *can* run away from your problems.

Fit for love

If better health, improved self-esteem, and increased life satisfaction are not good enough reasons to exercise, then maybe the promise of a better love life will entice you. I can point to many reasons why this is so. The most obvious reason is that a better appearance will make you more attractive to the opposite sex. You didn't need me to tell you that. But what about the physiological aspects of exercise as it relates to your experiences in the bedroom?

Here are the facts. Exercise increases bloodflow to the genitals, which is essential to both men and women becoming aroused, and to men having and sustaining an erection. It also optimizes nerve function, heightening the body's ability to sense or feel. Furthermore, exercise increases testosterone output which increases sexual drive for both men and women. Additionally, being fit means having more strength, endurance and agility in the bedroom....enough said.

All this being said, I believe the psychological benefits produced by regular exercise have a more profound effect on one's sex life. Exercise boosts self-esteem, improves body image, and reduces stress, which are all factors relating to sexual dysfunction and sex drive. As you might have guessed, countless studies have been done which prove this to be true. And if you need more proof, try experimenting yourself. It might be fun!

Energy for living

There are so many wonderful things to enjoy in life. Unfortunately, with work and/or school, family commitments, housework, and the like, most of us don't have any energy leftover to enjoy our moments of leisure. If this situation sounds familiar, exercising may be the last thing on your mind. Ironically, however, if you lack energy, exercise should be one of your first priorities. That's because regular exercise can boost the body's energy levels so that you can make the most out of your leisure time.

Although any physical activity is good for the body, aerobic exercise is a must for general health, particularly if you want to have more energy. Aerobic exercise can be defined as an activity involving continuous rhythmic movements, preferably lasting at least 15 to 20 minutes. Running, walking biking, and swimming, to name a few, are all aerobic activities. Tennis, basketball and racquetball are not purely aerobic because they are "stop-and-go" activities. Weight training, gardening, and cleaning, however are generally not considered aerobic.

I'm sure if you ask people who have recently started exercising, they will confirm that their energy levels have increased. But, I bet you are curious as to how this happens, right? Firstly, exercise boosts energy levels because it decreases stress, anxiety and depression, all of which are the most common causes of fatigue. Secondly, exercise elevates mood and provides a sort of natural high by releasing hormones called endorphins. High spirits usually translate into high energy. Last but not least, regular aerobic exercise improves the cardiovascular system, which results in more efficient oxygen transport to the brain. Of course the impact of exercise on cardiovascular function is vastly more complicated than that, but I prefer to keep it simple.

Despite all the science, it is impossible to quantify how much energy a person may have at any given time. Therefore, it's hard to gauge the exact impact exercise has on each individual's energy level. What we do know is that everyone responds differently to training. On one hand, I have known people who have cut their sleep requirements in half within a few weeks of starting an exercise program. Incidentally, their quality of sleep usually improved as well. There are others that see more subtle improvements with regard to energy. For instance, they may still need the usual eights hours of sleep per night, but have more pep to get through the day. The only way of knowing to what extent exercise can improve your particular energy levels is to experience it yourself. Hint, hint!

Obesity: more than skin deep

Approximately 60% of Americans are overweight and 25% are obese. Those statistics are alarming, especially considering the fact that being overweight is not just an aesthetic problem. On the contrary, having a serious weight problem can be deadly. People who are considered 20% or more overfat have a mortality rate that is almost 3 times greater than those of normal body composition.

This is the case predominantly because obesity often leads to diabetes and/or hypertension, each of which substantially increases the risk of stroke and heart attack. It's also important to note that the fatter one becomes, the more precarious his situation becomes. The risk of having a stroke or heart attack increases as the proportion of body fat increases.

Obesity is truly becoming an epidemic and needs to be taken very seriously, even by those who feel healthy otherwise. For those with chronic illnesses unrelated to body composition, being overweight is especially dangerous because it can only exacerbate their existing health problems. Fortunately, losing weight is not an impossible task when you have the proper guidance. In the pages ahead, I offer that guidance. The valuable tips and information provided in the following chapter can help anyone, disabled or not, lose weight and achieve his or her fitness goals.

Chapter Eleven
Take Action

Golden Rules

Over the years, I have developed guidelines that I give to my clients in order to make their lives easier. These "golden rules" will help you avoid common pitfalls on the road to becoming fit.

Training

Have fun

What's the most effective exercise you can do? Many years ago, I heard fitness expert, Covert Bailey give the perfect answer to this question: "The one that you will do." Exercise should be as fun as possible, so don't suffer through a kickboxing class if you prefer swimming. Find the things that are most appealing to you because if you dread your workouts, you will be less likely to continue.

The truth be told—most aerobic exercises are more or less similarly effective. Whether you do the treadmill, stationary bike, or stairclimber, you are ultimately the one burning the calories, not the machine. Granted, as a rule, jogging requires a higher caloric expenditure than bicycling. But if jogging hurts your knees for instance, or you just hate it for no good reason, you will put less time and effort into the workout. On the other hand, if you love cycling, it makes sense that you will be more inclined to exercise longer and harder. So do what you like, and if you don't like anything, do what you dislike the least.

The talk test

Many people who exercise fail to adequately tax the body. For instance, let's say you try to get your exercise in by walking with your friends. If you have absolutely no problem carrying on a free-flowing conversation, you are not working hard enough. Yes, you should be able to talk when walking at a low intensity, but not as easily as if you were sitting on your couch. Remember, you are supposed to be walking, not strolling.

If you go to the gym at all, you have probably heard the term "fat-burning zone." Many trainers will tell you to do your aerobic exercise at a slow pace to burn more fat. Supposedly, when you exercise more vigorously, you are no longer in this zone for optimal fat burn. Unfortunately, many people—trainers included—are confused on this issue. It is true that the body burns a higher percentage of fat during low-intensity aerobic exercise. For instance, the body might use 70% fat and 30% sugar during a brisk walk, while the percentage might be 50/50 during a run. But the body burns the highest *percentage* of fat during rest. Does that mean one can lose weight by sitting on the couch all day? No, because even 100% of zero is still zero. The bottom line is that the more vigorous the exercise, the higher the calorie burn, and consequently the higher the total fat burn.

Here is an example: 70% of 100 calories expended during a walk is still only 70 total fat calories burned. Conversely, if you run, you might be burning only 50% fat, but the caloric expenditure of running is obviously a lot higher than walking. So 50% of let's say 200 calories expended during a run is 100 total fat calories burned. Exercise with this in mind, and forget about all the fat-burning zone mumbo-jumbo.

Another advantage of working harder is that it takes the body a long time to recover after intense exercise. This is the period of time in which you may be resting, but your body will be working hard to recover. And this recovery requires the body to expend many more calories than it would after low-intensity exercise.

Vigorous exercise is also important if your goal is to strengthen your cardiovascular system. The quickest and most efficient way to strengthen your heart and lungs is through high-intensity exercise. Of course everyone has different limitations, so a slow jog may be quite intense for many people. Furthermore, if you have a health issue related to the cardiovascular system, intense exercise may not be recommended.

When you take everything I mentioned into consideration, along with the fact that increasing exercise intensity decreases the length of the workout, you can see that sometimes working harder is working smarter.

Interval training

This type of training is the quickest and easiest way of employing aerobic exercise to get fit. I'll use jogging to explain how it works. You start by walking briskly for five minutes to warm up. Then, you start jogging at a slow pace for three minutes. At the end of the three minutes, jog faster for a one minute interval. For this minute, carrying on a free-flowing conversation should be impossible. When the interval is over, slow the pace down for another three minutes, or until the talk test can be adhered to. Repeat the cycle a few more times. The harder you work during those one minute intervals, the faster you will get fit and lose weight.

I used to employ interval training with my clients for two basic reasons. The first reason is that it fights boredom. Interval training keeps you engaged in the workout and helps break up the monotony of a long, steady pace. Secondly, it is a very effective mode of training that allows one to train at high intensities, while still staying in the infamous "fat-burning zone." I highly recommend this form of training, especially for people who want to lose those last few stubborn pounds or train for an athletic event.

Time of tension

If you want to increase your strength or muscle mass, resistance training—lifting weights, calisthenics, or anything similar—is a must. For resistance training to lead to significant muscle development, the working muscle must be under constant tension for an adequate period of time. Thus, two things must be kept in mind. The first is that each repetition must be performed deliberately—slow on the way up and slow on the way down. Always remember that you are not in a race—keep it slow. The second consideration is the number of repetitions performed. Most experts, including those at the National Strength & Conditioning

Association, feel that 8-12 repetitions (it should not be easy to complete) is the appropriate range for optimal muscle development. However, falling outside this range is not a bad idea, occasionally.

Vary everything

The body adapts very well to external stressors such as exercise. Therefore, with regard to resistance exercise, try to vary things like grips, spacing, and rest periods. Varying your grip is as simple as putting your hands close together while doing bicep curls, and putting them farther apart the next time you do curls. Similarly, you can vary the spacing of your feet while doing squats, for example. One day you would have your feet close together, toes pointing forward, while the next squat day you would use a wide stance with toes slightly pointing out. Mixing up your rest periods in between sets—the time you normally spend gabbing—is beneficial as well. According to the National Strength & Conditioning Association, rest periods should be approximately one minute for maximum muscle growth, but can be paired down to 30 or 45 seconds once in a while. Only power-lifters benefit from longer rest periods, usually lasting between three and five minutes.

Varying aerobic exercise is easier because there are so many activities one can take part in. But if you are a sucker for one particular activity, such as bicycling, interval training is the best way to vary the routine. One day you can do one minute bursts, followed by three minute "rest" periods (meaning slowing the pace,) and the next workout day you can do 30 second, maximum effort bursts followed by four minute "rest" periods.

Something is better than nothing

When you are tempted to neglect exercising because you don't have the time or energy to make it worthwhile, think again. Thinking that a little exercise is akin to no exercise at all is the biggest mistake you can make. Ten minute workouts are not a waste of time—I do them all the time! Being consistent is much more important than the length of your workouts.

I met a woman a few months ago who subscribed to the all-or-nothing theory of fitness. That is to say that if she didn't have at least 90 minutes to workout, she didn't even bother. Of course finding a block of that much time is not easy, so she worked out twice a week at the most. In total, she exercised for 3 hours per week, but she wasn't seeing any results. When I told her to reduce her total workout time to 2 hours per week, but to break it up into six 20 minute sessions, she was very resistant. Despite her insistence that my suggestion wasn't logical, she humored me by going along with it.

Well wouldn't you know it, the guru—that would be me—was right again. Despite putting in 33% less time at the gym, she dropped down to her target weight within weeks. How, you ask? Well, first of all, with only 20 minutes to exercise, she made the most out of her time by exercising vigorously. Before, she was pacing herself too much in order to get through the entire 90 minutes. Motivation was also a key factor. When a person is tired or stressed, a short workout seems much more palatable than a 90 minute marathon session. There may even be other reasons for her success, but the fact remains—short workouts work!

Making sure to get your exercise in, no matter how brief

or light, is especially important for those with a disability. If you allow your particular disability to force you into a sedentary lifestyle, your health problems will be compounded. Unfortunately, it is very easy to fall into this trap. Even with my vast experience in fitness, I let my condition stop me from exercising. Instead of doing whatever I could do, I did nothing. For many people with physical limitations, simply moving around the house is sufficient exercise. For people like Christopher Reeve, even having others move your limbs for you is beneficial, as he has surely proven.

Diet

Water

You've heard it a thousand times: Drink 8-10 glasses of water a day. And I bet you've ignored it a thousand times too.

Maybe the one thousandth-first time will be the charm. Proper hydration is an integral part of optimal health, fitness, and performance. Drinking enough water is pretty much a no-brainer, so I will just make one comment. Cooler water rehydrates the body quicker than warmer water because it empties from the stomach faster. This is important if performance in an athletic event is an issue. If you are trying to drink water before a meal to prevent yourself from "pigging out," warm water is preferable. This is because warm water stays in the stomach longer, and makes you feel more full.

Eat and be merry

By far, the most difficult task I've encountered as a trainer is trying to convince people that eating more—especially more often—is the way to increase metabolism and lose fat pounds. No matter what, some people insist on skipping meals. Yes, these are the same resistant thinkers I mentioned in Part II of the book. The fact is eating 5-6 small meals a day is the best way to get lean.

Over the years, I have learned that the best way to turn these lost souls away from the "dark side" is to offer an example: Sumo wrestlers. A Sumo's main goal is to gain weight, and become as fat as possible. Do you think then, that these wrestlers eat all day long? On the contrary, the typical Sumo eats only twice per day. These meals are extremely high in calories, specifically carbohydrates. To contrast this example, let's examine the eating habits of the professional bodybuilder. Their main goal is to get their body fat level as low as humanly possible. As you might have guessed, virtually all bodybuilders eat at least 5 balanced meals a day. So, I ask you, which example do you want to follow?

Meatball with that spaghetti?

Carbohydrates are the body's primary source of energy. When consumed, carbohydrates, especially simple sugars, are metabolized rather quickly. What this means is that if you are sitting on your butt after eating a carbohydrate-rich meal, your body will have a lot of energy (calories) with nothing to do with it. Consequently, the calories are stored as fat.

Combining a protein with a carbohydrate serves to slow down this metabolic process, providing the energy from the calories over a longer period of time. No excess energy all at once means no need for fat storage. It's a similar process to that of time-released vitamins or drugs. These time-released tablets contain an amino-acid wrapped around the particular drug or vitamin. The tablet therefore breaks down slower, and is available in smaller amounts over a longer period of time.

So my advice is to reduce your carbohydrate portions, and add a protein. Some suggestions are: Add meatballs to pasta; add beans to rice; add chicken to salad; add yogurt to banana; add cottage cheese to toast; etc.

Conclusion

Full circle

When I was a kid, my nickname was "bag of bones." So, as you could imagine, as a skinny teen-ager, I had a real complex about my body. My chest was so indented that it gave new meaning to the term chicken-chest. However, I was extremely athletic, excelling at every sport that I tried. And at age fourteen, I intended to excel at bodybuilding. Little by little, I started filling out. By the time my eighteenth birthday rolled around, my nickname had changed to "the house." I didn't look like a football player because I am small-boned, but I had muscles popping out in every direction.

At that time, I was working out three hours a day, six days a week. For three hours each day, I was a man possessed, working out with tremendous intensity. Guys at the gym used to think I was nuts. This, coupled with going to school, working, and socializing, required a lot of energy. And I had plenty to spare.

The gym where I trained was replete with hard-core body builders. A couple of guys took me under their wing, and taught me quite a bit. I appreciated the knowledge I was given and gladly passed it on to others. That's when I decided to become a personal trainer. I studied exercise physiology in school and became a Certified Strength and Conditioning

Specialist—the elite certification amongst conditioning coaches, athletic trainers, and fitness specialists. Eventually, I started training most of my personal training clients in their homes. I loved my job, especially when clients were seeing life-altering improvements to their bodies.

But at 25 years of age, I developed Parkinson's Disease.As I continued to help grateful clients improve their bodies, my own body was breaking down. With every passing year, I looked, and felt, like less and less of a trainer. My decline was rapid. Two years ago, at age 32, I could barely do a pushup. Even things like taking a short stroll were exhausting. At 6 feet tall, I weighed a sickly 145 lbs. My loved ones thought I was at death's door. I tried to workout, but I didn't have the energy, the motivation, nor the ability to exercise. I tried every remedy known to man to try to feel better.....nothing helped. I had the expertise to help people transform their bodies, but now, I couldn't even help myself.

I guess you could say I came full circle—back to the bag of bones I was as a kid. But luckily, I still possessed the fire in my belly and the will to excel. It wasn't easy to change my skinny little body way back when, and it sure wasn't easy the second go-round either—but I succeeded. Considering my Parkinson's Disease, my body is in the best shape it's ever been. I've gone from weighing a paltry 145 pounds to a solid 175 pounds, and have gone from barely being able to do a few pushups to bench pressing 275 pounds. Alright, so they don't call me "the house" anymore, but that's certainly okay with me.

The objective

I hope with all my heart that you can benefit in some way from what I've written. After all, that's precisely the objective. When I originally embarked on my mission against despair, my plan was solely a matter of self-preservation. But as my ideas started to take shape, I recognized this as a golden opportunity. This was a chance for me to pass something on to my son—my thoughts, my ideas, and my experiences. My words would be something that he could hold on to, forever. It was my hope to provide him with both, a source of inspiration, and an affirmation of my love, even after I'm long gone. After all was said and done, I thought maybe, just maybe, someone else out there could benefit from my work. That possibility gave me great pleasure. At the very least, I hope that somewhere between the covers, you have found some inspiration, hope, strength, wisdom or humor to help make your life just a little brighter.

As for me, I'm still defying despair. It has been a tough road, but the journey has made me mentally and emotionally powerful. And physically, I feel better now than I felt five years ago. Yes, it's true; after all the blood, sweat, and tears produced from my fight against despair, I still have Parkinson's Disease. But at least *it* no longer has *me*!